Angora Cat

The Angora Cat Owner's Manual

Angora Cat Facts and Descriptions, Choosing and Acquiring, Feeding, Grooming, Breeding, Training and Behavior Modification, Showing and Other Care Requirements All Included!

By: Lolly Brown

Copyrights and Trademarks

All rights reserved. No part of this book may be reproduced or transformed in any form or by any means, graphic, electronic, or mechanical, including photocopying, recording, taping, or by any information storage retrieval system, without the written permission of the author.

This publication is Copyright ©2021 NRB Publishing, an imprint of Pack & Post Plus, LLC. Nevada. All products, graphics, publications, software and services mentioned and recommended in this publication are protected by trademarks. In such instance, all trademarks & copyright belong to the respective owners. For information consult www.NRBpublishing.com

Disclaimer and Legal Notice

This product is not legal, medical, or accounting advice and should not be interpreted in that manner. You need to do your own due-diligence to determine if the content of this product is right for you. While every attempt has been made to verify the information shared in this publication, neither the author, neither publisher, nor the affiliates assume any responsibility for errors, omissions or contrary interpretation of the subject matter herein. Any perceived slights to any specific person(s) or organization(s) are purely unintentional.

We have no control over the nature, content and availability of the web sites listed in this book. The inclusion of any web site links does not necessarily imply a recommendation or endorse the views expressed within them. We take no responsibility for, and will not be liable for, the websites being temporarily unavailable or being removed from the internet.

The accuracy and completeness of information provided herein and opinions stated herein are not guaranteed or warranted to produce any particular results, and the advice and strategies, contained herein may not be suitable for every individual. Neither the author nor the publisher shall be liable for any loss incurred as a consequence of the use and application, directly or indirectly, of any information presented in this work. This publication is designed to provide information in regard to the subject matter covered.

Neither the author nor the publisher assume any responsibility for any errors or omissions, nor do they represent or warrant that the ideas, information, actions, plans, suggestions contained in this book is in all cases accurate. It is the reader's responsibility to find advice before putting anything written in this book into practice. The information in this book is not intended to serve as legal, medical, or accounting advice.

Foreword

Before you consider bringing an Angora cat or kitten into your family home, it is essential that you take the time to learn everything you can about the breed so you can decide whether it is really the right choice for you. In this guide, you will learn the basics about the Angora cat breed including key facts and a breed history. After reviewing the information in this book, you should therefore have a better idea whether or not the Angora is the right cat for you and your family.

Included inside this book's first section is about the descriptions and facts about an Angora cat. It also contains information about its history, appearance, personality behavior, and lifespan.

The Second section is about choosing and acquiring an Angora cat. It tackles things to consider before getting an Angora cat and how to select a healthy one.

Th third section will talk about how to prepare for your Angora cat. It will discuss the supplies that you will need and a guide on how to prepare your home for the arrival of your Angora cat.

The next section focuses on how you can cater your Angora cat's nutritional needs.

The fifth section will talk about how to properly groom your beloved pet.

In the next part, you will learn how to train and interact with your Angora cat. It also includes a guide on its behavior modification.

The seventh section focuses on the common health issues of an Angora cat and how to deal with them.

The seventh section is a guide on how to show your Angora cat- how to prepare and how it will be judged in show.

For the last section, it will talk about the breeding process for your Angora cat.

Start learning about this wonderful animal on the pages that follow. And although you should never view a single source of information as a comprehensive guide, you should be better prepared to care for an Angora cat after finishing this book.

Table of Contents

Introduction 1

Chapter One: Angora Cat Facts, History, Descriptions and Characteristics 3

Chapter Two: Choosing and Acquiring an Angora Cat 9

    Selecting Your Kitten 9

    Prices: Top Dollar Or Value Buy? 10

    Questions To Ask About The Breeder 10

        Breeding Contract 12

    How to Check If an Angora Kitten is Healthy 12

Chapter Three: Preparing for Your Angora Cat 15

    Supplies Needed 15

        Kitty Litter Box 16

        Bedding 17

        Scratching Posts 18

        Food Bowl 19

        Toys 19

        Grooming Kit 20

        Collar and Carrier 20

    Preparing Your Home 21

        Look for Possible Dangers 21

        Where To Keep Your Cat 25

Where To Put Everything 26

The Indoor or Outdoor Question 28

Chapter Four: Feeding Your Angora Cat 31

Types of Food 32

Dry Foods 32

Canned Food 33

Semi-moist Food 34

Food for Pet Cats 34

Vitamins and Minerals 36

Frequency of Feeding 37

Chapter Five: Grooming Your Angora Cat 39

Trimming Claws 40

Brushing 42

Hairballs 43

Bathing 44

Chapter Six: Training and Behavior Modification 47

Litter Box Training 47

Keeping the Litter Box Clean 49

Teaching the Cat to Use the Cat Door / Flap 49

Training Your Cat to Respond to Commands 51

Basic Training 52

Your Angora Cat's Name 52

Fetch 53

Getting Down 54

Sit on Command 55

Sit-Stay 55

Standing Up 56

Understanding the Clicker 57

Asking Angora Cat to Come 58

Hush 59

Shake 60

Hold-Paw 61

Go Somewhere 61

The Names of Things 62

Take 63

Leave 64

Leash-Heel 65

Clicker Training for Your Cat 66

Cat Misbehaviors and Causes 71

Soiling Outside the Litter Box 72

Spraying Urine 73

Destructive Chewing 74

Destructive Scratching 74

Excessive Vocalization 75

    Aggressiveness 76

    Jumping Where They Shouldn't 76

  Traveling with Your Cat 77

Chapter Seven: Vet Care for Your Angora Cat..................... 83

  Vaccinations 84

  Flea and Tick Medication.. 84

  Vitamins 85

  Spaying and Neutering 86

  To Declaw or Not to Declaw? 87

  Exercise 87

  Signs of Illness 88

    Behavioral Signs 88

    Physical Signs 90

  When to Visit a Vet 91

  The Veterinarian.. 92

  How to Find a Good Vet 94

  Cat Insurance 95

  Common Feline Diseases 98

Chapter Eight: Showing Your Angora Cat............................ 117

  Preparing For Show 117

  What Is The Description Of An Angora Cat To Show?.. 118

  How are Angora Cats judged in show?............................ 118

The Angora Cat Pedigree 119

What To Prepare If You Want To Enter Your Angora into A Cat Show: 119

TICA Angora Cat Standard 120

Chapter Nine: Breeding Your Angora Cat 123

Things To Remember When Breeding Your Angora Cat 123

Reproduction 124

Pregnancy 127

Childbirth 128

Raising Kittens 130

Artificial Feeding 131

Conclusion 133

Glossary of Cat Terms 135

Index 145

Photo Credits 149

References 151

Introduction

The Turkish Angora is a very special breed of cats that differs significantly from many others. There are many elements in cat training that are equally valid for all breeds. However, each breed has special characteristics and traits that make them unique. And it is precisely these characteristics that are important in cat training.

Some educational elements are much more important, more difficult or easier with your Turkish Angora than, for example, with a British Shorthair and this is exactly what I will point out to you again and again on the following pages. The training methods for all breeds are often similar, but you will always receive advice from me if you have to pay attention to something special about the Turkish Angora breed. But now it is important that you get to know your Turkish Angora and its peculiarities exactly.

Let's get started!

Chapter One: Angora Cat Facts, History, Descriptions and Characteristics

The breed of the Turkish Angora is one of the oldest in the world, as it was first mentioned in the 16th century. According to legend, even the prophet Mohammed is said to have owned a cat of this breed. Her name, on the other hand, is a little misleading about her origin. Angora is the old name of today's Turkish capital Ankara. However, experts suggest that this unique breed originally came from the Caucasus.

Those same experts have also found out that the Turkish Angora is one of the few semi-long-haired cats that have obtained their coat length through natural mutation and

Chapter One: Angora Cat Facts, History, Descriptions and Characteristics

not through selective breeding. For this reason, she is often referred to as the great mother of all long-haired cats.

It was also her beautiful silky fur that made her known throughout Europe and made her a status symbol. Because in the 16th century the sultans of the Ottoman Empire sent the Turkish Angora as gifts to the courts in England and France.

Although it maintained its status as a court cat for a long time there, it was overthrown from its throne by a new breed towards the end of the 19th century. The rise of the Persian cat resulted in such a depleted population of Turkish Angoras that even the zoos in Ankara and Istanbul began keeping specimens to ensure their continued existence. The export was banned and only allowed again in the 1980s. Since this went hand in hand with the recognition by the FIFe (international umbrella organization of cat breeding associations), nothing stood in the way of worldwide breeding.

Compared to their ancestors from the 16th century, today's specimens are much smaller and slimmer. Nevertheless, the Turkish Angora, with its 25 cm shoulder height and up to 5 kg, is one of the medium-sized cat breeds. Your physique is muscular, but at the same time should appear graceful and fine. It is elongated, which looks very elegant due to the slender legs. The paws should be small and delicate. Because the fur has hardly any undercoat, it is tight and does not become matted quickly. It's half-length, smooth and silky.

Chapter One: Angora Cat Facts, History, Descriptions and Characteristics

Since this breed has adapted ideally to the hot summers and cold winters in the Caucasus, the fur becomes particularly dense in winter and forms both a plush collar on the neck and thick trousers on the hind legs. The tail is very bushy all year round and does not lose its fullness even in summer. The most common color in the Turkish Angora is still white. Originally only this color was allowed. But since pure white is based on a genetic defect that is unfortunately often associated with serious damage to health (such as deafness, imbalance or blindness), this restriction has been dropped. Only in Turkey itself is only white allowed as a color. In all other countries, all colors except for Chocolate, Fawn, Lilac and Point are permitted.

But despite this genetic disposition, the Turkish Angora is an extremely popular breed, and that's a good thing. Because she is very sociable, extremely friendly and approachable in every form. Another impressive feature of this breed of cats is their attachment to and orientation towards humans. In stark contrast to other breeds, a Turkish Angora shows quite openly that it does not like to be alone and prefers to follow its people at every turn. Even going for a walk and fetching games, as most people only know from dogs, is quite possible and not uncommon with a well-behaved and trained Turkish Angora.

Turkish Angoras are also very intelligent and attentive and are extremely interested in what is happening in their immediate vicinity. Due to their playfulness, these clever little animals learn some things faster than their owners would

Chapter One: Angora Cat Facts, History, Descriptions and Characteristics

like. For example, it is not uncommon for Turkish Angoras to open doors independently or turn taps on and off, although they were never consciously taught to do so.

This cat breed not only gets along well with children and other animals, but also shows genuine interest and a great willingness to play. She rarely or never shows aggressive behavior, which is why she is also well suited for families with small children. She endures the hustle and bustle with a calm and serenity that she also likes to transfer to her owner.

With regard to her posture, she has only minor demands and is very frugal. It can be kept completely as an indoor cat. She is never averse to a garden, as she enjoys observing nature and she does not reject one or the other hunting adventure. However, it does not have to be an outdoor cat to lead a satisfied and balanced cat life. However, if you want to give it space to run, I only recommend it in a fenced garden, which is best also spanned by a net. This not only ensures that your Turkish Angora does not escape, but also that all birds and other small animals are safe from it. In addition, it is not suitable for a real outdoor walker, as it is far too people-friendly. She would go with other people without hesitation and let herself be pampered. Due to their appealing appearance, it is not uncommon for Turkish Angoras to unintentionally change hands as a result.

Much more important for your Turkish Angora than access to the outside world is the closeness, the time together and the loving interaction with you and all other people and animals in the household. It is important for them to

Chapter One: Angora Cat Facts, History, Descriptions and Characteristics

participate in family life and be integrated into activities. Whether it takes place inside or outside is completely secondary for your Turkish Angora.

If you have not yet selected your Turkish Angora, but are still thinking of buying one, I would like to give you the following tip: Obtain it from a reputable breeder and find out more about him and the parent animals. Your Turkish Angora will happily live to be 12 years or older, so it is important that she is well positioned in terms of health and social background and that she will not have a difficult life from birth due to overbreeding. Also, take a close look at how the breeder treats their own cats and whether this is in line with the methods you will learn in this book. A cat traumatized in early adolescence requires an enormous educational program and that is overwhelming for most cat owners. A reputable breeder should always be able to show you the pedigree. No ancestor may appear twice here in order to avoid inbreeding problems from the start. Even if it can hurt, a seriously bred Turkish Angora often costs around 800 euros. Everything that is significantly lower should arouse your suspicion, as these are usually so-called multipliers. They place little value on species-appropriate keeping and good socialization of their animals, and certainly not on a healthy genetic basis.

Take a close look at the kittens as well as the breeder and the parent animals before buying, so that your happy life with your Turkish Angora is not put in the way from the beginning.

Chapter One: Angora Cat Facts, History, Descriptions and Characteristics

Of course, you can also adopt your Turkish Angora from the animal shelter at any time. This option would not only be very classy and exemplary, but you would also give the cat the chance of a good, fulfilled and happy life at the same time. However, not everyone is ready or able to take in an animal shelter cat, as these cats rarely come into the home without previous stresses. These can be of a health nature, which may burden you financially for the entire life of the cat, or the little velvet paws have had traumatic experiences and are therefore perhaps even behavioral and difficult to convey.

Both do not have to apply, but the possibility is much higher with a shelter cat than with a cat from a reputable breeder. You should be aware of this and address all risks and possible previous burdens in detail in the animal shelter. If you feel up to this challenge, it is great that you are giving a shelter cat a new home! For the upbringing of your Turkish Angora, this probably means that you have to be more patient again and plan a few more repetitions for many things in order to overwrite old experiences and behavior patterns. But with the right attitude and the firm will you will also succeed, I am convinced of that.

Chapter Two: Choosing and Acquiring an Angora Cat

Selecting Your Kitten

When the time comes and you have made your decision to select a Turkish Angora kitten to be the newest member of your family, it's important to note that most breeders will have kittens available for sale somewhere between 12 and 16 weeks of age. Don't trust a breeder who is offering you a kitten that's younger than 12 weeks because it's not safe nor healthy for the kittens to leave their mother that early. After 12 weeks of age, most kittens will have had their

Chapter Two: Choosing and Acquiring an Angora Cat

natural inoculations and their first set of shots, and the ability to adapt to a new home.

Prices: Top Dollar Or Value Buy?

Pricing on a pure-bred Turkish Angora kitten will usually vary a couple hundred dollars from breeder to breeder. The top-of-the-line breeders will charge more because their cats are highly sought after by other breeders and wealthy clients. They charge around $700-$1,000. On the low end, you can pay a couple hundred but be **careful** when buying from an unexperienced back yard breeder. It's important that you do your homework on your breeder to avoid the harsh reality that some have experienced of paying for a Turkish Angora and getting a different breed entirely. Don't encourage amateurs buy supporting a lousy operation. You do usually get what you pay for in the Turkish Angora world. Prices will vary from region to region, do some research online to see what they are going for around you before agreeing on a price.

Questions To Ask About The Breeder

- *Are the kittens caged up?* If so, they may be less socialized and backwards.

- *Can you see the parents?* If not, they're hiding something.

Chapter Two: Choosing and Acquiring an Angora Cat

- *Can you see pictures of other Turkish Angoras they've bred?* Most breeders should have plenty to show you.

- *Has the breeder ever won any shows?* Always a plus.

- *Do they have free reign of the house?* If so, they will be more socialized and trusting.

- *Is the breeder's home clean?* If it's dirty, avoid doing business with them.

- *Does the breeder provide Turkish Angora genetic lineage documentation?* Any reputable breeder will.

- *Is the kitten at all sick in anyway?* If so, do not buy. Regardless of what the breeder says.

- *Are the kitten's eyes blue?* If not, stay away. They should be either teal or royal blue depending on whether you are looking for a TICA Thai or Modern.

- *Is the kitten frail?* Turkish Angora will be on the frail side. They should be energetic though.

- *Are there an excessive amount of kittens in the household?* There shouldn't be more than one litter perhaps two but any more than two litters is a red flag that this breeder is in it only for money

Chapter Two: Choosing and Acquiring an Angora Cat

Breeding Contract

If you plan to breed your cat down the road, don't sign a breeding contract which requires you to have your kitten fixed within 6 months of purchase. Check the coat, color points, eye-color, body structure, and overall look of the kittens before you decide.

How to Check If an Angora Kitten is Healthy

Of course, you will want to check if an Angora kitten you are considering taking home is not just emotionally healthy, but also physically healthy. First, ask to see veterinarian reports from the breeder to satisfy yourself that the kitten is as healthy as possible, and then once you make your decision to share your life with a particular kitten, make an appointment with your own veterinarian for a complete examination.

Before you get to this stage, however, there are a few general signs of good health to be aware of when choosing a healthy kitten from a litter, including the following:

- **Breathing** – a healthy kitten will breathe quietly, without coughing or sneezing, and there will be no crusting or discharge around their nostrils;
- **Body** – they will look round and well fed, with an obvious layer of fat over their rib cage;
- **Coat** – a healthy kitten will have a soft coat with no dandruff, dullness, greasiness or bald spots;

Chapter Two: Choosing and Acquiring an Angora Cat

- **Energy** – a well-rested kitten will be alert and energetic;
- **Hearing** – a healthy kitten with good hearing should react if you clap your hands behind their head;
- **Genitals** – a healthy kitten will not have any sort of discharge visible in or around their genital or anal regions;
- **Mobility** – a healthy kitten will walk and run normally without wobbling, limping or seeming to be weak, stiff or sore; and
- **Vision** – a healthy kitten will have bright, clear eyes without crust or discharge and they should notice if a ball is rolled past them within their field of vision.

Chapter Two: Choosing and Acquiring an Angora Cat

Chapter Three: Preparing for Your Angora Cat

Before your most current cute little Angora cat shows up in your home, you should be completely ready for their appearance. This implies setting up the fundamental devices, for example, collars, transporters, feline litter boxes, and toys. Here is an agenda of all the gear that you will require for preparing your textured pet.

Supplies Needed

Chapter Three: Preparing for Your Angora Cat

Remember that you don't generally need to get them at the same time, you can simply begin with a couple of things first and contribute all the more once your feline has grown up. Furthermore, recall that having the correct instruments is simply a large portion of the fight.

While preparing your feline, you ought to inject energy, love, and devotion with the goal that you will end up being a more successful coach.

Kitty Litter Box

One of the benefits of having a feline rather than another sort of pet is that they just go potty on one explicit territory. Be that as it may, this can likewise be a twofold edged blade because their propensity is difficult to break.

This implies on the off chance that they chose to drop their bomb on the floor covering, anticipate that they will do these on various occasions. To keep your home spotless, you should give your kitty his own litter box.

While picking a litter box, there are a few factors that you have to consider. The first is size. On the off chance that your house is little, there are a ton of boxes that element space-sparing plans. Notwithstanding, you ought to likewise think about the size of your feline. Ensure that they have adequate space for their legs to loosen up.

Another factor to consider is the style. Essentially, a feline litter comes in two normal shapes – an open plate and

Chapter Three: Preparing for Your Angora Cat

a shut plate. The previous is accessible in changing profundity. Yet, as its name infers, it doesn't have any spread, which implies that it may not be reasonable for modest pets.

The shut plate in the interim accompanies a removable cover. Different items even have a fold entrance produced using sturdy textures.

You can likewise get self-cleaning feline litter boxes available. Even though they are new, these items are picking up notoriety as a result of their accommodation to the proprietor. Tragically, these self-cleaning gadgets are just promoted to the pet proprietor, and not to the feline. These items produce irregular commotions and developments that may alarm your feline while he is doing his business.

To make it simpler for you to clean the kitty litter without deflecting your pet from utilizing it, you can get one that is produced using polythene. Some litter plate additionally has antiperspirants to add flower newness to your place.

When finding an area for the feline litter, you have to put it in a prudent territory that is far away from food or water. Like people, felines like to do their business secretly.

Bedding

Obviously, every pet needs to have his own special happy with resting region. However, before you purchase a pet bed, you have to gauge your Angora first. This is

Chapter Three: Preparing for Your Angora Cat

significant because a ton of pets like to extend their legs while they are napping off.

Then again, there are additionally felines that like the sentiment of being supported. For this situation, you ought to get a little and rounder assortment.

Moreover, huge felines require denser pads to help their weight.

Scratching Posts

On the off chance that there is one thing that cats love separated from dozing, it's scratching. They will scratch the ANY surface that they find because the activity is now important for their inclination.

Driving your feline to end this propensity can be incredibly troublesome and tedious. The most ideal approach to manage this issue is to give your feline a scratching post where he can sink his paws in.

Most importantly, the scratching post must be steady and sturdy. Even though their paws are pretty much nothing, they can join the post truly hard, particularly on the off chance that they are super eager to play. An item with an elastic base can help improve dependability.

The post ought to likewise be tall. As a general guideline, the scratcher ought to be at any rate 30 inches tall to oblige felines everything being equal.

Chapter Three: Preparing for Your Angora Cat

Food Bowl

A treated steel food plate is a most loved decision among most veterinarians since they are anything but difficult to clean. You can likewise utilize glass bowls since they are non-permeable and it doesn't leave a trailing sensation to pet food. It is likewise dishwasher-safe, making it simpler to clean.

Plastic food bowls, then again, ought to be kept away from if conceivable. Truly, they are modest, yet these items represent a lot of danger to your pet. If the plastic bowl becomes scratched, it can hold perilous microbes. A ton of plastics likewise contains BPA that is referred to for setting off ailments, for example, malignancy and cardiovascular issues.

Toys

Preparing your catlike buddy will doubtlessly be simple on the off chance that you have toys nearby. A wad of yarn, a noisy toy, or even a laser pointer can give long periods of fun and amusement for your catlike companions. If you are utilizing the laser pointer, ensure that you don't point it straightforwardly on the feline's eyes as it could prompt visual impairment.

Chapter Three: Preparing for Your Angora Cat

Grooming Kit

Felines are commonly spotless all the time since they groom themselves. Be that as it may, they will value you more on the off chance that you additionally keep an eye on their requirements. First off, you need a search with metal teeth for unraveling their long hide and a bug brush.

For felines with incredibly long hairs, they additionally need a wire brush and slicker brusher. If you have the cash to save, you ought to contribute on a de-shedding instrument to abstain from tangling.

Collar and Carrier

In contrast to canines, it isn't generally that regular to walk your feline with a rope. Yet, for wellbeing purposes, you should at present give your pet a neckline that is anything but difficult to eliminate. This will enable a feline to escape effectively if his headstalls out someplace.

On the off chance that you are taking your hide ball someplace far, ensure that he is kept in a portable transporter. Besides guarding them, it likewise gives them a feeling of serenity while going out and about.

Chapter Three: Preparing for Your Angora Cat

Preparing Your Home

Preparing your home to welcome a new kitten is very much like getting ready to welcome a new baby into the home. After all, your little kitten *is* a baby. Yes, it may only be a baby animal, but it needs a safe environment to grow in, just like a human baby does.

If you were bringing home a human baby, you would be looking at your home, removing any hazards, and putting certain things out of harm's way. You would be finding a safe place to put their cot, away from loud noises and bright lights. You would be working out where to keep their food and nappies and toys and generally preparing the home ready to receive them. Bringing home an Angora kitten is no different.

Look for Possible Dangers

Go around your home, starting at the front door, and look at everything as if you are a visitor seeing your home for the first time. It is surprising what you see when you look at things from this perspective.

Things that are normally invisible to you because of familiarity suddenly stand out as in need of obvious attention. Look for clutter that needs to be put away. Look for anything that could potentially fall over if knocked. Look for anything that a kitten could get tangled up in. Look for small things lying around that could be chewed or swallowed, for example, coins, hair-clips, pen lids, guitar picks, etc. Basically,

Chapter Three: Preparing for Your Angora Cat

look for anything that you would not let a small child play with.

You may need to reconsider where certain items live and find new homes for them, like in cupboards or on higher shelves. You might need to consider replacing open bins and waste paper baskets with closed-top ones.

You should pay special attention to wires and electrical cords. We have multiple gadgets and devices in our lives these days, and our homes are filled with all kinds of phone chargers and laptop cables, and electrical cords. You might need to consolidate some of these into a neater arrangement and use cable organizers or cable boxes.

Initially, your sweet little kitten will be sticking to the floor or low-set furniture like the sofa. So the things you have on your dressing table or around the bathroom sink should be okay for now. But by about 6 months of age, kitten will have grown sufficiently to jump up onto most surfaces around the home. At that point, you will *have* to look at how you store all those various perfumes and lotions and creams that you don't want the cat getting into, so it might be worth looking at that now anyway. Cats often delight themselves in being able to knock items off a surface with their paws, and you don't want to come home to find your expensive bottle of perfume smashed on the bathroom floor.

Recliner Chairs

Chapter Three: Preparing for Your Angora Cat

The humble recliner chair is not something obvious that you would immediately think of as dangerous. After all, it is something that makes your life easier and more pleasurable. But this luxurious item that is bringing comfort and ease to *your* life is a whole world of danger for your kitten!

Angora cats love to get underneath things and into tight spaces, and you will always find them crawling out from underneath furniture. So if you are not aware that your kitten is sleeping under your chair when you operate the recliner mechanism, it could have very dire and tragic consequences.

If you have a recliner, the one simple rule is: make sure you KNOW the whereabouts of your kitten before operating it, either up or down.

So my advice is that it's best to moderate your use of your recliner for a little while, at least until you get used to having a cat around.

If you have an Electric Recliner, I recommend unplugging it from the power outlet for a while so that you don't operate it absent-mindedly, at least until you get used to sharing your home with a pet. Or, if you have a Manual Recliner, try taping a piece of cardboard onto the handle to act as a reminder whenever you go to operate it without thinking. That way, you are going to keep Kitten safe, and at the same time, train yourself to always be aware of the cat before reclining into your favorite position.

Chapter Three: Preparing for Your Angora Cat

Once you have got used to having a cat around all the time, you can plug your Electric Recliner back into the power outlet, but still take it easy and stay aware.

Houseplants

Something you definitely need to check is the types of plants you have in your home. Why? Well, because some plants are poisonous to Angora cats, especially Lilies.

Any plant in the Lily family can cause problems, but some are worse than others. Easter Lily, Tiger Lily, and Stargazer Lily can cause kidney failure if a cat eats any part of the plant. So you need to make sure that you remove any Lilies or any plants you suspect might be Lilies.

If your Angora cat is allowed outside, you should also check your garden and make sure you remove any Lilies from there too. In the long term, you also need to make sure that any flower arrangements you bring into the home do not contain Lilies.

Note, if your cat does get exposed to Lily poisoning, you cannot treat them at home. You will need to take them to a vet as soon as possible.

Chapter Three: Preparing for Your Angora Cat

Where To Keep Your Cat

Once your new cutie has settled-in as part of the family, they will most likely have the run of the house, but that is a few weeks away yet.

When they first come to your home, you will want to restrict them to a smaller portion of the premises, if you can, so that they are not overwhelmed as they try and get used to a new environment. So, depending on the layout of your home, you should consider whether you have an area that can be closed off from the rest of the house for a little while.

I am not talking about just one small room, like a utility room, but rather a couple of rooms or a small section of the home. For example, if you have a living area that can be closed off from the bedrooms by closing a door or two, that would be ideal.

You should also be looking at whether that area can be closed off at night, even after they have settled in. That way, they can occupy the whole house during the day but be restricted to that smaller area whilst you are asleep. This is because you don't really want your small kitten running about the hallway and bedroom area when you get up to go to the bathroom in the middle of the night. You could be at risk of treading on them or mistakenly shutting them into the bathroom or your bedroom without realizing it.

Chapter Three: Preparing for Your Angora Cat

Where To Put Everything

There are three things you need to consider the placement of carefully: (i) the feeding bowls, (ii) the litter tray, and (iii) the cat bed.

If you have identified an area that can be closed off for them at night, you need to place all three of those items within that area because you don't want to shut-off access to their bowls or litter tray at night.

You also need to think about whether the initial placement is where you plan to keep each item in the long term. Once your kitten has got used to where things live, you don't want to confuse them by regularly moving things around. If you keep moving the litter tray, for example, they may get confused as to where they need to do their business, with unfortunate results! So try and keep things in the same place if at all possible.

If you do have to move it, try not to do it too often, and make sure you take the time to show your kitten where it has moved to.

Bed

Ideally, the bed should be tucked away somewhere cozy, like under a coffee table against a wall; or in a corner down behind the TV. Your cat will probably not use it all that much, preferring to sleep on your sofa or favorite armchair during the daytime. But when they do want to get away from

Chapter Three: Preparing for Your Angora Cat

it all, they need to feel like they have a cozy, safe place to retreat to. So if you can make it feel like the bed is in a dark little cave, they will love it and be more likely to use it.

Bowls

The food and water bowls should be placed on the opposite side of the room to the litter tray (because none of us like to poop where we eat!). You want to make sure that they are out of the line of foot traffic so that no-one is accidentally knocking the cat as they walk past when they are trying to eat. If the area is carpeted, you would be wise to put down some kind of tray or mat to place the bowls on. That would help define the feeding area and also catch any spills of food and water, keeping them off your lovely, clean carpet.

Litter tray

The litter tray should be placed in a corner, rather than along the middle of a wall. It needs to feel like a secure, safe place so that the cat doesn't feel vulnerable and develop any anxiety issues about using the litter.

When your cat uses the tray, they will cover-over their business with the loose fresh litter by flicking it up with their paws. So having it surrounded by two walls also helps inhibit the spread of any litter that gets accidentally kicked out of the tray as they do so.

Chapter Three: Preparing for Your Angora Cat

You should set-up the litter tray before you first bring your kitten home, as this will be the first place you show them when they arrive. Put a fresh liner in, and fill the tray to a depth of about an inch and a half, or roughly 3cm to 4cm. Your kitten will be used to using litter by this age and will instinctively know what to do with it.

The Indoor or Outdoor Question

One of the things you need to decide before you bring your Angora cat home is whether you are going to allow them to go outside or whether you want them to live indoors full-time.

If you have never owned a cat before, you might not realize is that they are not always calm, docile animals that lounge around all day like Garfield. They are natural hunters in the wild and have a hunting instinct even when they are hand-fed and live indoors in a soft-furnished home. So there are certain times each day when your calm, peaceful kitten will turn into a madman.

The hunting instinct will kick in; their eyes will go big, their ears will stick up, and off they go, tearing around the house in a frenzy, like kids on a sugar rush. Running from room to room, leaping onto the furniture, they race around, just wanting to get all their energy out in one quick burst. Then 10 mins later, they are back to the usual cat's life of sleeping, watching TV, and sleeping some more. This

Chapter Three: Preparing for Your Angora Cat

behavior can be a little surprising if you are not expecting it, but it is all part of the feline charm.

So, deciding whether you want to allow them out of the house for that hunting playtime is a crucial decision to be made up-front. Once you take the cat home, it has to be either allowed free access to roam outside or be trained to stay indoors all the time. You can't go back and forth between the two

Neither way is right or wrong; it is simply your choice. Personally, I like to keep cats inside, but that is just my preference. Overall, you need to consider what will work best for you in your circumstance and what availability you will have to look after your cat. At the end of the day, if you have small children running in and out of the house into the backyard all day, there might be little chance of getting your cat to stay in all the time.

When Angora cats are allowed to roam freely outside, however, they are more at risk, being exposed to the possibility of worms, ticks, and fleas, and also to poisonous plants. Outdoor cats are more likely to get into "hissing" fights with other cats, and tiny kittens can also be at risk from natural predators such as foxes and birds of prey.

However, always remember that the main danger to any Angora cat is of human origin: - the dreaded automobile! You can't teach a cat how to cross a road safely using a pedestrian crossing, so they are always at risk of getting hit by a car. If you do allow them outside, you might find it desirable to

Chapter Three: Preparing for Your Angora Cat

invest in some kind of pet insurance to help cover vet bills, if needed.

One more thing to be aware of is the situation with the local by-laws where you live. Some local councils have rules about not letting cats out at night since they see them as feral pests that hunt and kill the local native fauna. Most counties will have some kind of pet registration procedure, but some may also have a curfew requiring cats to be kept indoors after a particular time in the evening.

So, make sure you check to see if your local council has a cat curfew or other rules about letting cats roam free. You may have to make sure that your cat is indoors at night.

Once you are sure that you have got everything ready, it is time to bring your Angora cat home. Let the kitten-parenting begin!

Chapter Four: Feeding Your Angora Cat

Now, let's move on to one of the most important aspects of caring for your Angora cat– his diet. You have to know exactly what you should feed your cat as such will ensure that you will be giving him the right foods all the time, particularly those that meet his nutritional requirements and needs based on his age, activity level, and lifestyle.

Kittens and cats need a higher percentage of protein than dogs, i.e. about two times more and they require more fat as well. Best sources for protein supplementation are meat, eggs, fish 'and milk. Milk is a good source of calcium while egg yolk and cooked egg is good source of protein, fat and vitamins. Excessive feeding of meat, chicken, fish can be harmful as it may cause poor eyesight, stunted growth, lack of calcium and Vitamin A. Cats should never be fed with chicken bones. Water should be available all the time.

The senses of smell and taste in cats are closely connected, as they are in all mammals. Distinctive to cats is the absence of response to sweets, and hence cats avoid all foods that taste sweet.

Types of Food

Pet food industries have developed very well in the last few years. Researches have been done to develop the food with different raw products and flavors to meet the demand of an animal's body. These are readily available food instead of preparing fresh food for animals. That is why these are preferred by the owners. Mainly three types of foods are available in the market.

1. Dry food
2. Canned food
3. Semi-moist food

Dry Foods

These are available in different flavors containing meat, fish, vitamins, preservatives, fat, cereals and coloring agents. The long-term use of this type of food may cause urinary problems as water content is lacking in these products. So, nutritious food, which is juicy enough to fulfill water requirement of Angora cat, should be given along with dry food. The combination is beneficial for the Angora cat to meet all its requirements.

Adult cat and kitten need different protein and fat requirement i.e. diet should contain at least 25 per cent protein for adult and 40 per cent animal protein for kitten while 25 per cent fat concentration is important. The remaining part contains cereals and vegetables. Angora cats should be fed 14 g for every 0.45 kg body weight. Angora cat's appetite can be checked. When after eating food, cat cleans its whiskers and goes to sleep, it depicts that the given food is enough.

Canned Food

This food is available in cheaper and costlier varieties. Cheaper canned food contains maximum portion of either, meat or fish, which are not useful to meet the cat's requirement, whereas costly food contains meat or fish in proper concentration. These products should be processed and stored, opened and used safely. These are processed at very high temperatures and after processing care is taken to add Vitamin B as it gets destroyed due to heat. It is always important to note the ingredients to know the nutritive value of the product.

Semi-moist Food

These types of foods are highly palatable and nutritious and contain meat, vitamins, preservatives and chemicals to provide attractive color to foods. The label should be checked for packaging, as their storage life is limited.

Food for Pet Cats

Pet cats, which are indoor animals, are dependent on owners for food. Unlike the free cats who have free access for the type of food. 80 owners have to take care to provide all the nutrients otherwise by giving only one type of food, the cats will develop the problems because of deficiency of vitamins and minerals.

Meat

Raw meat should be minced and cooked, baked or steamed to prevent the natural juices. Liver is good for cat but excess feeding will cause diarrhea. Heart can also be given occasionally. Lungs and spleen may cause diarrhea.

Chicken/Poultry

This can be given in cooked form. Precaution should be taken not to feed the bones as boiling makes them sharp and can cause internal damage.

Fish

Chapter Four: Feeding Your Angora Cat

Sea fish with dark flesh and oil are most useful for the cat. Fish bones should not be fed, as these are harmful like the poultry bones.

Eggs

Egg yolks may be given either raw or cooked Egg White should not be fed much as it may inhibit the absorption of Vitamin BZ.

Milk

Most of the cats enjoy milk. Some cannot digest the lactose present in milk and may have digestive problems. Cats who are fed only milk receive less Vitamin A and fat, so, cod liver oil should be supplemented along with the food.

Water

Water should be always available and changed at least three times a day.

Cereals and Vegetables

Cereals including bread, corn flakes can be mixed with milk or meat or fish. In Vegetables cooked potato, cabbage and carrots can be fed.

Salt

It can be added occasionally to change the taste of food.

Vitamins and Minerals

The pharmaceutical industries have developed the various additives with food industry, which can be supplemented. But their excessive use in diet is harmful as they may cause other complications like bladder stones, rickets, etc.

The following Vitamins are important:

- Vitamin A-It is important for growth and can be supplemented by using egg yolk, liver or cod liver oil.
- Vitamin B-It helps in growth, heat functioning and nervous system and can be obtained from yeast, egg yolk and liver.
- Vitamin D--This acts as catalyst for the absorption of calcium and phosphorus. Main source for this is sunlight and cod liver oil.
- Vitamin E-This is related with fertility and can be supplemented by wheat germ oil.
- Calcium and Phosphorus-These two minerals are required for bones in growing animals and for the absorption of other nutrients. Sources for these are red meat, milk and other foods. If the cat is supplemented with various diets, it does not need these additives.

Loss of Appetite

Angora cats go off feed because of multiple reasons. One reason could be breeding season and second reason can

Chapter Four: Feeding Your Angora Cat

be unwashed bowls or stale food. Third possible reason can be unpalatable food. Fourth reason can be that neighbors have fed the cat and owner is unaware of this fact. Sometimes cats may have problem in teeth or other oral lesions or may be the indication that cat is having some problem. If it is so for more than twenty-four hours, then the cat should be taken to veterinarian for checkup. Dry food contains very less water, fat and proteins. So, cats on dry food should have plenty of water as they may have urinary bladder problems. To prevent these problems, one should feed canned food or semi-moist food as cat will get used to other foods and will have a balanced diet. Dry foods help in preventing the buildup of tartar and will keep the teeth clean.

Canned foods contain higher percentage of protein, fat and water than other foods and are easily palatable. The nutrient supplements should be checked to give a balanced diet to cats and always make sure that food is at room temperature and is not fed directly from the refrigerator.

Semi-moist foods are almost nutritionally complete for cats but not for kittens. They are cheaper as compared to other foods because they contain vegetable proteins as well. Water contents are higher in comparison to other foods but water should be always available.

Frequency of Feeding

The quantity and frequency of food depends on age, weight, activity and breed. Kittens should be fed more

Chapter Four: Feeding Your Angora Cat

frequently than cats as they cannot withhold large quantity of food if fed only once in 24 hrs. Thus, they should be fed more frequently with less food and let it have the food and then remove the bowl from there.

Chapter Five: Grooming Your Angora Cat

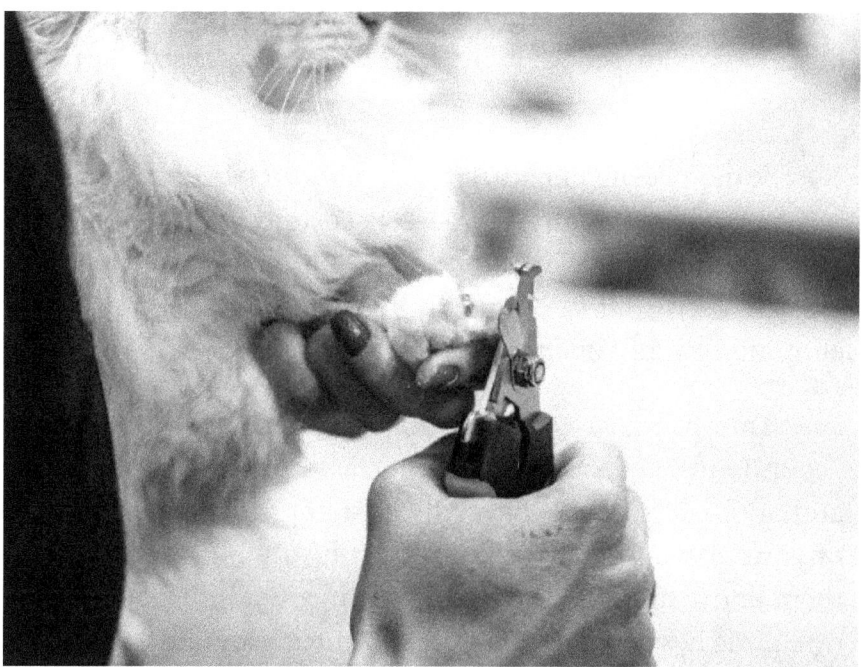

Grooming is not just an important part of keeping your Angora cat fun to snuggle and looking cute—it's also important for their overall health and a great way to build trust with body handling. This section will cover basic grooming recommendations to keep your Angora cat's skin, coat, claws, and nails in tip-top shape.

Chapter Five: Grooming Your Angora Cat

Trimming Claws

Claw trimming is an essential cat-care task, especially if you have children. After all, you don't want your little ones heading off to school with big cat-scratch marks up their arms.

Some people get scared of having to trim cat claws, but it is an easy task really, and it gets easier the more you do it. Start trimming regularly when your kitten is young, and they will get used to it very quickly. You will find that they need clipping roughly every two weeks.

The primary skill to use when trimming claws is "confidence." If you try and trim claws while feeling nervous and apologetic, the kitten will resist and try and wriggle out of your arms. But if you hold them firmly but gently and let them know that you are in charge, they will relax and let you do it. It is best to choose a quieter time, though, don't try and do it when they are all playful and energetic because they will not want to sit still for you.

The best method is to sit them on a table in front of you, holding them between your arms but against your body, so that they are facing away from you. Then use one hand to take hold of a paw and gently squeeze the paw to expose one claw at a time. Simply slip the nail clippers over the curved white portion of the claw and clip it. When you look closely, you will see a darker core in the middle of the claw. Be careful to only clip the white part, and stay well away from the darker part. Cat claws are just like human fingernails: if you clip only the white part, you are fine, but if you cut too close to the

Chapter Five: Grooming Your Angora Cat

quick, they can bleed. If you do happen to clip the darker part and cause bleeding, don't worry; just dab with a tissue, and it will stop in a few minutes.

Failing that, if you find you are just unable to get them to sit still and submit to being clipped, there are two other options open to you:

1. Get the vet to clip their claws for you. This may seem the easiest because you don't have to do it yourself, but it does mean all the hassle of having to book-in an appointment, get the cat to the vet, etc. Most vets will be all too happy to clip your cat's claws for free as part of a scheduled visit for a check-up or some other issue, but if you are booking an appointment just to get claws clipped, they may charge a fee.
2. The other easy option is to try and clip your kitten's claws while they are asleep. If your cat likes to fall asleep on your lap in the evenings, this could work out well for you. Just keep the clippers close to your armchair, and choose your timing well. The cat needs to be in that zoned-out, deep sleep stage of their nap. If they are not deeply asleep, you are likely to wake them by clipping. Even though they are sleeping, try and maneuver them gently to get access to their paws without being too rough and waking them.

Chapter Five: Grooming Your Angora Cat

Brushing

Cats are naturally self-cleaning creatures that love to groom themselves and keep themselves meticulously clean. On a day-to-day basis, they will lick their coat to remove dirt and any loose hairs. They seem to do a pretty good job of it all by themselves, but they appreciate any help you can give them by brushing them regularly. Brushing your Angora kitten is something you should start in the first few days so that they get used to it from an early age.

When you brush your Angora cat, do it gently as if you are petting and stroking them. They will be very inquisitive about the brush at first and will want to sniff it and probably bite it before they let you use it on them. Let them. Let them get familiar with it so that they trust it when you bring it near them.

Start at the top of the head between their ears, and brush smoothly down along their back. They may not like it at first and keep trying to turn around and grab the brush, but that is okay. Once they get used to gentle strokes down the head and along the back, they may let you brush their sides and even their tail as well. As they get more familiar with brushing, they will come to enjoy it and enjoy the interaction with you. However, they will need to get very comfortable with the whole process before they let you get the brush anywhere near their tummy.

Your Angora cat will need more brushing at the start of summer because they will molt and shed hair to have a lighter, cooler coat for the warmer months.

Chapter Five: Grooming Your Angora Cat

Hairballs

When Angora cats lick themselves, the loose hairs get swallowed and should pass through the digestive tract with no problems. However, if your cat swallows a lot of hair, they may have difficulty digesting all of it, and it can accumulate in the stomach as a hairball.

Angora cats usually don't get problems with hairballs when they are a kitten because their hair is shorter and thinner. But when they are adults, their hair is thicker and harder to digest. Also, longer-haired breeds are more likely to swallow much more of it and require brushing far more often to prevent hairballs.

When an Angora cat does develop a hairball, it deals with it by vomiting it up. This may come as a shock the first time you see it. Your Angora cat will start making strange noises and start convulsing their body as they retch and try to eject the hairball. Don't be alarmed; it's a natural process: they might look like they are in distress, but they are not. Once they get it up, don't scold them, even though you now have a small icky mess to clean up with a piece of paper towel. Instead, congratulate them and praise them for doing a good job!

Chapter Five: Grooming Your Angora Cat

Bathing

You don't need to bathe your Angora cat unless they accidentally get covered in something that will be too much of a cleaning job for them to handle themselves. For example, if they go outside, they might get covered in mud, which they cannot lick off by themselves. Or even inside the home, they might manage to get covered in something that needs to be washed off, especially if you have younger children that like to play with them (tomato sauce on a cat, anyone?)

Bathing an Angora cat is relatively simple but is not something they would naturally enjoy. So, you just need to keep them calm and keep reassuring them throughout the procedure so that they don't freak out and try and jump out halfway through, scratching you in the process.

What you need:

1. Sink, or bath, or large bucket – a plastic baby bath is ideal
2. Cat shampoo – not human shampoo, which could irritate them
3. Towel – a good size to wrap them up in afterward
4. Face Washer or washcloth
5. Plastic jug - for rinsing them

Chapter Five: Grooming Your Angora Cat

Method:

Fill the bath or sink with warm water, not too deep and not too hot. Just deep enough to cover their legs if they were standing, and just warm enough to feel inviting and relaxing, without any risk of feeling too hot and make them want to jump out. Just like a baby's bathwater, test the temperature with your elbow.

1. Gradually lower the cat into the water, letting them get used to it until they are sitting in it, being held gently, but firmly, by you.
2. Use the jug to gently pour water over their body to wet all their fur, but avoid pouring any on their head, face, or ears.
3. Squirt a small amount of cat shampoo on to them and massage into their fur to produce a soapy lather. Work your way all over their coat, being careful with sensitive areas.
4. Then rinse off with more water from the jug, being careful to remove all the suds so that they are not left licking shampoo off themselves later on. You might want to have a spare bucket of clean, lukewarm water on hand to rinse with so that you are not just rinsing the shampoo back onto them from the water they are sitting in.
5. Wet the face washer and squeeze it out before using it to clean the face, head, and ears gently. Be careful, as

Chapter Five: Grooming Your Angora Cat

their whiskers are very sensitive, and they may not like you touching them.

6. Once Kitten is clean, you can lift them out of the water onto a nice big clean towel on your lap. They will love being wrapped up in a towel after a bath, just like you do. Make a fuss of them while you towel them off, and let them know how good they have been. Getting them towel-dry should be enough. As long as they don't feel too wet, they should be okay to finish the drying process naturally themselves. Remember, cats in the wild get wet in the rain and manage to dry off okay, all by themselves.

Afterward, let them wander off and find a quiet place to relax and recover from the ordeal. For most Angora cats, having a bath is a two-edged sword: on the one hand they don't like the experience of being wet, but on the other hand, they love all the attention and fuss they get from you. But they will probably still want to go and get some "alone time" to reflect on the experience.

Chapter Six: Training and Behavior Modification

Contrary to the belief of others, Angora cats could actually be trained—just like dogs! Here are a few good things to start with.

Litter Box Training

Elimination disorders are common among Angora cats that aren't trained. In fact, these are one of the most common problems for which most pet owners seek veterinary advice.

Chapter Six: Training and Behavior Modification

Basic knowledge about Angora cats can help you prevent litter box accidents right in the beginning when you bring your kitten home. Angora cats have a natural instinct to use sand or soil for elimination purposes, and kittens start to use litter box as early as four weeks of age. However, make sure the litter box is easily accessible for the kitten. It should not be placed in a noisy or inaccessible place.

When you bring your kitten home, immediately take it to the litter box and place it inside, gently taking their front paws teaching them how to scratch at the litter.

Set the Angora cat up in this manner every day - place it in the litter box at different intervals when a cat would normally go to release itself – immediately as it gets up in the morning, after play time, after meals, and after waking up from a nap.

Leave the kitty alone when it is using the litter box, as most cats prefer privacy at this time.

However, in the event of any accidents, it is important that you do not punish your kitty. Yelling will only cause greater confusion, besides scaring your cat. Moreover, it won't understand the reasons for your anger.

Instead, use an enzyme cleaner to clean up the area and to remove stains. Continue to place your cat in the litter box until it starts to use it on their own.

Chapter Six: Training and Behavior Modification

Keeping the Litter Box Clean

Angora cats are finicky about cleanliness, as they are clean creatures. It is important that their litter box is cleaned regularly; or else, your kitty may start to avoid using a dirty, filthy litter box.

- Regularly change the litter once a week.
- Scoop it at least once every day.
- Avoid using a strong-smelling disinfectant
- Rinse the box well after cleaning & washing.
- Clean any pet stains with an enzyme cleaner.

Teaching the Cat to Use the Cat Door / Flap

Most Angora cats can easily learn to use the flap even without training. However, some do require training. It will help to introduce the flap to your cat even before installation. Give it a chance to inspect it on its own and get used to the sight and smell

When it comes to installing the cat door, it is important to consider the distance from the feline's belly to the floor. Additionally, make sure that the flap opens up into a sheltered area, rather than an open space. It is likely that cats may feel apprehensive of being ambushed in open spaces.

If you are installing the flap in an open location, make sure you place objects, including benches, pots, around the flap, giving your kitty ample space to hide behind if they feel vulnerable stepping out into the open space.

Chapter Six: Training and Behavior Modification

Once you are done with installation, start training your kitty in how to use the flap. What's better than a treat or reward? Cats love treats, so you can use different rewards to encourage your kitty to start using the cat flap.

However, if it is still hesitant to use the new cat door, you may want to add their scent to it. They are more likely to trust something that has their own scent. You can do this by wiping its face with a cloth and then using the same cloth to wipe the cat flap.

The cat door is likely to make a sound upon opening and shutting. Sensitive cats may not like this noise and try to avoid the flap. Push the flap gently. This will ensure that there isn't too much noise to frighten your cat. Reward it when your cat is happy to use the flap. This is important to tell your cat that a treat is on its way if the cat successfully uses the flap, without feeling disturbed or frightened.

Prop the flap open with a peg or piece of tape to create a more inviting hole, which is easier to pass through for your kitty. Before removing the prop, make sure your cat gets enough time to getting used to using the flap. Do not lose patience if your cat takes a long time to getting acclimatized to the flap.

Chapter Six: Training and Behavior Modification

Training Your Cat to Respond to Commands

Like dogs, cats are trainable, though cats aren't motivated by praise as much as dogs. Obedience training is one of the most crucial parts of Angora cat training.

You can make your Angora cat do what you want it to do with persistent hard work and practice. It all begins with finding what motivates your cat the most. Of course, food is a big motivator for everyone, and cats are no exception.

Tasty treats can be used as baits to lure your kitty to come to you. Bringing in a variety of treats will help to keep things interesting for your cat. Reserve the treats for the time when you call your cat.

Then you may want to select some unique words that you plan to use only when you call your kitty. It is best to avoid using its name when you are calling it, since you would be using the name in other contexts as well. This may confuse your cat.

Consider using the terms "Come here," "Treat time" or any other such terms that you can use often to call your kitty. It is a good idea to use a clicker or whistle for calling your kitty. When it is at a short distance from you, use these terms to invite it to come closer. When it reaches closer, take a step back, and again call him or her to come closer.

Repeat the process and this will help it learn to associate responding to your calls with treats. The training

Chapter Six: Training and Behavior Modification

should be carried out indoors first and expanded to outdoors only when your kitty is responding positively to your calls.

Keep changing treats in between so that the kitty doesn't find the reward as boring and stops responding to your calls because the treat no longer interests it. Remember, coming to you should be a pleasant experience for it. So, make sure it is not related to the times when you are taking it to the vet, trimming its nails, or doing any other task that does not interests your pet.

Always end each training session on a positive note with a happy response from your Angora cat.

Basic Training

Your Angora Cat's Name

Of course, one of the best things you could teach your Angora cat is how to respond to his own name. It's always good when your Angora cat responds to his name because it is a form of recognition, and it makes him feel like he's not just an Angora cat, but that he's actually important, too.

Here's what you should do:

1. Call your cat by his name, and when he does not respond, ignore him.

2. Then, when he finally looks at you, go ahead and give him a treat.

Chapter Six: Training and Behavior Modification

3. Repeat, and say your Angora cat's name right before clicking. When he responds, give him a treat.

4. Repeat some more until he has no problems responding to his name anymore.

Fetch

Teaching your Angora cat how to bring something to you could also be helpful! This way, he could bring you the things you need. It's also fun for other people to see him bring something to his parent!

Here's what you should do:

1. Ask him to get something by using the said command, and once he does, coach him to come towards you.

2. You could lure the Angora cat with a toy so he'd come nearer. Then, use the clicker, and give him a treat.

3. Repeat until your Angora cat feels the need to bring you something even without command, and then use the command *Bring it.*

4. Try placing the toy on the floor, then go across the room from your Angora cat and say *Take it*. Once he has it in his mouth, say *bring* it, and see if he brings it to you. If he does, give him some treats, and don't forget to praise him!

Chapter Six: Training and Behavior Modification

Teaching your Angora cat how to bring something to you could also be helpful! This way, he could bring you the things you need. It's also fun for other people to see him bring something to his parent!

Getting Down

1. Show your Angora cat a treat while he's lying by your side, and then say *down.*

2. Then, bring the treat to the ground, and slide it towards him, so he would get it while lying down. When he's finally down, go ahead and give him the treat.

3. Then, try putting the treat in your right hand, and hold his collar with your left. Just hold it under the chin, and then say *down.*

4. Bring the treat lower while applying pressure to the collar. Say *down.*

5. Once the Angora cat lies down, go ahead and give him the treat, and praise him.

6. You can then ask your Angora cat to lie down even without the help of a treat. Just say down, and when he follows, go and give him a treat.

Chapter Six: Training and Behavior Modification

Sit on Command

One of the easiest tricks in the book, it's always good for a Angora cat to know how to sit on command. This is always best done with a treat—it easily reinforces the command to your Angora cat.

Here's how.

1. Lure your Angora cat with a treat over his head, and then say *Sit*.

2. After doing so, bring the treat over his eyes, and once he sits, go on and give him the treat.

3. You could also do another variation of this. Try putting the treat on one hand, then say *sit* while putting upward pressure on his collar.

4. Praise and pet him when he sits.

5. When he stands up, try saying *sit,* and show him the treat.

6. Repeat for around 2 to 3 times.

Sit-Stay

When it comes to obedience training, the Sit-Stay Command always comes in handy. It helps Angora cats stay

Chapter Six: Training and Behavior Modification

calm, and makes them understand that it's wrong to jump on people they don't know, or not to run around the house.

Here's what you should do:

1. Face the same direction with your Angora cat. It would be helpful if he's on your left side.
2. Attach the leash to his collar, and then make sure that the leash's loop is over the thumb of your left hand. Fold it in leash-accordion style, and make sure that the leash is close to the Angora cat's collar but that it is comfortable.
3. Apply some tension on the collar. Some people call this upward tension, and then say *Stay*.
4. After saying the command, come in front of your Angora cat, and keep the tension on the collar.
5. Count from 1 to 10, and then get back to his side.
6. Finally, release the tension, praise him, and then say *Okay*, and go ahead and move forward.
7. You can then increase the distance between you and your Angora cat. Do this only when he obliges to the *Stay* command all the time.
8. Another way to reinforce this command is by making sure that you tell him to *stay* once you get home from work and while he's greeting you.

Standing Up

Once you have taught your Angora cat how to sit, you can then teach him how to stand. This comes in handy when it comes to grooming him, and when you want him to walk with

Chapter Six: Training and Behavior Modification

you. A clicker could also help you out with this, but more on that later.

Here's what you need to do:

1. Ask your Angora cat to lay down, and upon standing up, use the clicker and give him a treat. It would then make him realize that he has done something good. Try to repeat this couple of times until he associates the act of standing up with getting a treat.

2. Use a verbal command (Stand) and a visual cue (your hand signaling upwards) so he would associate these actions with standing up.

3. And, try saying *Stand* while he's lying down. When he stands on command, go and give him a treat.

Understanding the Clicker

Clicker training is said to be one of the most effective methods of training one's Angora cat. It also proves to be efficient as it is used in a lot of commands, such as *Come*, and others that you'd learn about later.

Clicker training also resonates with treat-training. Basically, you'd give the Angora cat a treat once he responds to the clicker. To give you a better idea, read below:

1. Use the clicker, and then give your Angora cat a treat.

2. Repeat doing so for around 30 minutes. This way, the Angora cat would easily associate the clicker with

Chapter Six: Training and Behavior Modification

getting a treat, and of course, he would be excited for it.

3. Always remember the golden rule of clicker training: Don't ever click without treating, and never treat without clicking.

Asking Angora Cat to Come

One good way of applying clicker-training is to try teaching your Angora cat how to come towards you. This command is meant to help the Angora cat understand that you're his parent, and he should be obedient.

Plus, it might even save his life in times of emergencies. It's also best if you could practice it every day as it is one of those commands that could prove to be a core skill for your Angora cat.

Here's what you have to do:

1. Start the training by establishing the command. For example, say *Come baby,* or *Here Sweetie,* and then give the Angora cat a treat, and do not forget to praise him. Do this a couple of times in a day, and always give him a treat and some praises when he comes to you.

2. Then, stand across from your Angora cat, and say the command that you have been using. Once he comes, give him his treat, use the clicker, and give him several more treats.

Chapter Six: Training and Behavior Modification

3. Now, every time you want to call him, say the command, give him a treat, use the clicker, and give more treats.

4. You may also try petting your Angora cat once he comes to you, and then give him a treat. This way, he would not be ashamed of coming to you.

5. To advance in training, try asking him to come to you in various areas of the house.

6. Also, try calling him while he's doing something else (except when he's doing potty), and don't forget to give him his treats, praises, and pet him, too!

Take note that in case your Angora cat doesn't come right away, maybe you are using the wrong command, or he just could not relate to it. Try using a different command to call him, and it just might work.

Hush

Hush is another helpful trick because it helps your Angora cat keep quiet, especially when you're trying to talk to other people, or while you're doing something important. This is also great for when you have Angora cats who really bark too much.

Here's what you have to do:

Chapter Six: Training and Behavior Modification

1. While your Angora cat is barking, concentrate on him and then wait for him to look at you. Once he does, and if he stops barking, go and give him a treat.

2. Repeat a couple of times and then use the command *hush* before clicking and giving him a treat.

3. Then, naturally, while the Angora cat barks, go and say the command, click, and give him a treat when he obeys. Try to coax him into getting quiet longer and give him more treats.

4. Try adding a hand signal to stop him from barking, while still using the command and using the clicker.

Shake

This is a variation of Paw-Shake, where the Angora cat only shakes (not just his paw, but his body) when you ask him to.

Sometimes, Angora cats shake after being given a bath, or when he gets up after a nap. It would also be helpful if you could practice this trick once you see him shake (after a bath or so).

1. While he's shaking, use the clicker, and then give him a treat.

2. When he shakes again, use the clicker, and give him more treats.

Chapter Six: Training and Behavior Modification

3. Use the clicker and then use the command *shake*. Wait for him to shake, and when he does, give him some treats.

Hold-Paw

This trick is meant to teach your Angora cat how to shake hands with you. It's a good way of introducing him to other people, and it's always fun to see him shake your hand. Here's what you have to do:

1. Let your Angora cat sit in front of you, wait for him to lift his paw, use the clicker and then give him a treat.

2. Repeat this for around 4 to 5 times, and wait for him to lift his paw on his own. Use the clicker and then give him a treat.

3. Say *paw* every time he offers you his paw. Then, use the clicker, and give him a treat.

4. You can modify the session by giving the Angora cat treats only when he lifts his paws higher. You can help him do this by tickling his paw's hollows.

Go Somewhere

Next, it's time for you to teach your Angora cat how to go somewhere, usually a place marked by tape during training. It is a good way of helping your Angora cat get to bed, or sit down, especially when you are busy.

Chapter Six: Training and Behavior Modification

For this, you'll need a training stick. Here's what you have to do"

1. Let the Angora cat touch the training stick, use the clicker, and then give him a treat.

2. Put a disk or tape one part of the floor.

3. Point to the spot that you have marked using your training stick, click, and wait for the Angora cat to go to the said spot before giving him a treat.

4. Make sure to practice a couple of times until the Angora cat realizes that he has to go to that spot to get a treat.

5. Make up a name for the marker (i.e., *spot, mark, disk,* etc) while the Angora cat's about to step on it.

6. Use the clicker, give the Angora cat a treat, and then repeat process until such time that it's easy for the Angora cat to go to the marker upon hearing its name.

7. Try placing the marker anywhere in the room and see how your Angora cat reacts.

The Names of Things

Another amazing thing is that you could actually teach your Angora cat the names of various things around him. In fact, Chaser, a Border Collie, currently holds the record for knowing the names of over 1000 objects. This means that with proper training, your Angora cat might reach that level, too!

Chapter Six: Training and Behavior Modification

Here's what you have to do:

1. First, let your Angora cat touch your hand, and then use the clicker and give him a treat.

2. Place the object in your hand, say *touch*. Wait for him to touch the object but not your hand, and when he does, go and give him a treat.

3. While the Angora cat is touching the object, say the object's name—or however you want him to remember it. (i.e., *blankie, squeaky, bunny*, etc.)

4. Then, use the clicker and give him a treat.

5. Repeat for at least 4 to 5 times, then hold the object in your hand again, say the object's name, use the clicker, and give him a treat.

6. As for people's names, it would be helpful if you could use a training stick, point it to the person you want to introduce to your Angora cat, say that person's name, use the clicker, and give the Angora cat a treat.

Take

Yes, this is a command that will help your Angora cat pick something up from the floor. You could start with his toys, and then when he adapts the command, maybe you could ask him to pick your shoes up for you and the like.

Chapter Six: Training and Behavior Modification

Take note that you have to have a lot of patience when it comes to this trick because it requires some assistance. The results will be fruitful, so don't worry!

1. Place one of your Angora cat's favorite toys on a mat or on the ground.

2. Wait until he picks it up with his mouth (assuming it's his favorite, he definitely will go pick it up), and once he does, use the clicker and give him a treat.

3. Repeat until he picks up the toy without being hesitant or waiting for a long time.

4. Once he does that, use a command (*Get it, get your toy, take it*, etc), use the clicker, and give him a treat.

5. Try to point to various objects on the floor, and ask him to pick them up. Don't forget to use the clicker and give him a treat.

Leave

If you're going to teach your Angora cat how to take something, you also have to teach him how to leave things, too. This is essentially helpful during times when the Angora cat becomes too curious and wants to pick even dirty things off the floor. This way, you could prevent him from getting into harm, or acquiring germs, and the like.

Chapter Six: Training and Behavior Modification

1. Start training him with a biscuit. Leave a couple of pieces on the floor, call your Angora cat and say *leave it* or *leave*.

2. He would be tempted to take the biscuit, sure, but once he looks at you, go ahead and restrain her. Then, use the clicker and give him a treat. Don't forget to praise him, too.

3. Repeat the first two steps for around 3 to 5 times in a day.

4. Then, once your Angora cat learns the trick, you can then train him without the leash and with another treat or object on the floor.

5. Use the command whenever you see that your Angora cat wants to take something that he's not supposed to take, and that is bad for him. Don't forget the treats and praises!

Leash-Heel

To heel means to have your Angora cat walk beside you even without pulling him. This is great for times when you have to go out with your Angora cat, or when you want him to meet other Angora cats and people, too.

1. Loop the Angora cat's leash by the left side of your belt, and make sure you do not follow the direction where the Angora cat pulls the leash to.

Chapter Six: Training and Behavior Modification

2. Now, when your Angora cat moves closer towards you, use the clicker, and then give him a treat.

3. Next, since your Angora cat already knows how to walk beside you, say some commands while trying to get him close. Examples could be *Walk with me*, or *let's go*. You could also add his name there. These are definitely better than saying *heel!*

4. For every ten steps, use the clicker, and don't forget to give treats.

5. Try practicing for about 4 times each day, with each session amounting to around 10 to 15 minutes each.

6. You can begin training without the leash when you know that the Angora cat responds and walks with you all the time.

Clicker Training for Your Cat

Many people assume that cats want nothing to do with being trained or taught tricks and think they would be too stubborn to learn. However, most cats are very willing to learn and, with patience, you can correct their behaviors and teach them tricks.

Whether you are trying to correct your cat's behavior or teach it a trick, an Angora cat loves spending time with their human and can be easily trained. They are a very

Chapter Six: Training and Behavior Modification

intelligent breed and will easily learn what you are trying to teach them.

One of the best training methods to use for cats is clicker training. This type of training, more formerly called operant conditioning, uses a reward system to train cats, rather than punishment.

When you indicate a behavior that you want your cat to learn with a click, it should be given a treat when it repeats the preferred behavior.

The clicker used for training is a small plastic device that creates a clicking sound when the metal strip on the bottom of the device is pressed. The clicker is used because it is a distinctive sound that will generate curiosity the first time you use it. Voice commands can be added later, but in general, voice commands don't work well for training because they hear your voice every day and it usually doesn't generate curiosity in your cat.

When you start training your cat using the clicker, he or she will quickly associate a click with the behavior you want them to repeat. Once it has made that association, they will repeat the behavior when they hear the click. It takes patience to train a cat, so don't get too anxious if they don't respond to the first, or even the second, time you show it the behavior you wish for it to repeat.

This process is often referred to as "charging the clicker." Giving your cat a treat after they have repeated the

Chapter Six: Training and Behavior Modification

behavior will reinforce a positive consequence for their obedience, helping to make it easier to train.

Before you begin training, do some research online or buy a book that can help you get started with clicker training. Setting goals for your training is important as well. Decide which behaviors need to be replaced, which to encourage and decide if you wish to use the training to teach your cat tricks. Be reasonable when you set the goals and, above all, be patient as you begin the training.

The first step to clicker training is getting your cat used to the sound of the clicker. Since they need to associate the sound with a behavior, don't randomly use the clicker, use it only for training purposes.

Begin training by clicking it and immediately give your cat a treat. Be sure to use something they love to eat as this will help inspire them to participate in the training. Commercial cat treats work well for clicker training, but make sure they like the treats. When you give your cat a treat, you can either toss it to them or hand feed it to him or her.

Although it can take time for some cats to make the connection between the click and a treat, your Angora cat is very smart and they should make the association quickly.

Once your cat understands that if they respond to the clicker, they will be rewarded with a treat, you can begin them on more advanced training. However, don't start it unless

Chapter Six: Training and Behavior Modification

they have clearly made the association between the click and receiving the treat.

One of the easiest commands to teach a cat using clicker training is to come to you when they are called. Just as they would respond to the sound of a can opener, when you use the clicker, they will learn to come out of hiding in order to get their treat. The clicker can be useful when you cannot find them in the house and you need your cat to come to you.

Since the Angora cat is such a smart breed, you may also be able to teach your cat how to respond to visual and vocal cues. Use the clicker to teach them the behavior, then associate the visual or vocal cue with the clicker and treat. Repeat the process until you can replace the clicker with the visual or vocal cue, but remember to reward their repetition of the behavior with a treat just as you did with the clicker.

Timing is important when you use clicker training and you want to try to time the clicking with the preferred behavior and not click after it.

If you click after you cat has started doing the behavior, they may abruptly stop and expect to be rewarded with a treat. As you continue working with your cat, he or she should repeat the preferred behavior before they get a treat.

Don't use more than one clicks while you are training your cat or you could confuse it. In addition, do not play with the clicker between training sessions because not only do you

Chapter Six: Training and Behavior Modification

risk confusing them, but also, they will be disappointed when they don't receive a treat after you use the clicker. The treat is to keep them interested in training, so don't click if you don't intend to reward your cat.

Start your cat's training with something easy that your cat is likely to do on its own. If they nuzzle your hand, use their scratching post or sit down, click during the act and then give him or her a treat. Your Angora cat will quickly associate the behavior with the click and treat, then before you know it, he or she will repeat the behavior on command when they hear the click.

Keep each training session short so you don't get frustrated and your cat doesn't get bored. As they make progress toward the goals you've set for their training, be sure to reward them. Rewarding your cat as they make progress will let him or her know that it is doing the right thing and he or she will repeat the behavior in order to receive their tasty treat.

The key to training your Angora cat is patience and rewarding them. Angora cats love food and they are intelligent, which makes them easier to train than most other cat breeds. Once they have been taught two or three tricks, you can impress your family and friends with your well-behaved cat.

Chapter Six: Training and Behavior Modification

Cat Misbehaviors and Causes

Although the Angora cat is mild mannered most of the time, there are medical issues and circumstances that can cause behavior problems in even the most even-tempered breed.

There can be many causes for bad cat behaviors, including a rough beginning to their life, neglect, it can be a sign of aging, a dietary deficiency or it could be a sign that they are bored because they are left alone too much.

If your normally laid back cat suddenly develops behavior problems, make an appointment with your cat's veterinarian to eliminate physical ailments that might be causing the problems. By eliminating a physical reason for their behavior, you can concentrate on retraining your cat in order to correct the problems they are having. Retraining cats isn't difficult and the Angora cat's intelligence helps to make it even easier to accomplish. Some common cat behavior problems include:

- Soiling outside the litter box.
- Destructive chewing or scratching.
- Excessive vocalization.
- Aggressiveness
- Jumping where they are not allowed.

It is important to observe and get to know your cat's traits so you can notice changes in their behavior right away. If it is due to a medical condition, then you can get them help as soon as you are aware of the problem. The

Chapter Six: Training and Behavior Modification

sooner you get them treated the better, as some illnesses can quickly prove fatal to cats.

Some of these behaviors will develop as a cat gets older, as they can suffer from senility much like humans. If you adopt an older cat, they may have behaviors that caused their previous owners to give them up, but by retraining them, along with patience and love, you can correct their bad behaviors.

Soiling Outside the Litter Box

Urinating or defecating outside of the litter box is the number one reason that many cats are surrendered to animal shelters and it may be one of the easiest problems to solve.

If your cat suddenly starts to eliminate outside of his or her litter box, you should try cleaning it out more often. Cats will refuse to use a dirty litter box and start eliminating nearby it if they deem it too smelly or unclean. Cats have a great sense of smell and if they think their box isn't clean enough, they may eliminate next to their litter box.

If the litter box is frequently cleaned, there could be a medical reason that they are choosing to eliminate outside of their litter box. A urinary tract infection may cause them to urinate outside of the litter box because they cannot make it there in time. If they have hemorrhoids or if they are constipated, they may defecate somewhere other than their

Chapter Six: Training and Behavior Modification

box. If you notice these problems despite having a clean litter box, make an appointment with the vet to have your cat examined for medical issues.

Spraying Urine

Cats can be very territorial, especially with other cats they do not like, and they will mark their territory outdoors by spraying urine on it. However, if they are spraying indoors, it could be that they are marking their territory or it could be a sign of stress. Although Angora cats are very adaptable, cats don't always respond well to changes. Cats can be stressed by the addition of a new pet or baby to their home and moving to another house could stress them out, especially if the cat had previously been surrendered to a shelter. An illness of a pet or human family member can also cause them stress.

If there have been recent changes in your household and your cat starts spraying, try to reassure him or her by lavishing your cat with extra attention. Once they know that everything is back to normal, the behavior should stop. You will also need to eliminate the urine odor by using an enzymatic cleaning product. These products neutralize the bacteria that cause the odors to help eliminate them. If the odor isn't dealt with, your cat will keep returning to the same spot and continue to spray.

Chapter Six: Training and Behavior Modification

Destructive Chewing

There can be several causes for destructive chewing and you should be concerned by the behavior. Some of the items your cat chooses to chew on could be harmful for them or they may choose something that you value to gnaw. Some of the common reasons for excessive chewing are teething in kittens, boredom, curiosity or it could be a sign of a diet deficiency.

To help end destructive chewing, make sure you are feeding your cat a healthy, balanced diet in order for them to remain healthy and active. If your kitten is teething, give them a large straw to chew on, they will also find it fun to bat around and carry from place to place. Discourage chewing on cords, which can be very tempting for cats, and houseplants, as many of those are poisonous to cats. Use something to make them taste bad, such as apple bitter or gently spraying them from a water bottle will discourage worst behaviors.

Destructive Scratching

Supplying your cat with plenty of scratching surfaces doesn't mean they will leave your furniture and carpets alone, although it will help to reduce the odds of them using those surfaces for their primarily scratching needs. Scratching acts as exercise for your cat, helping them relieve stress and it keeps their claws maintained. Having scratching pads, scratching posts or even a large log will help to keep your cat away from your furniture and rugs.

If they do start scratching on your furniture or carpets, discourage their behavior with a short squirt of water from a spray bottle, trim their nails, or if the situation warrants, use nail caps.

Declawing a cat should never be considered, as that is like cutting off their fingers. A cat uses their nails to grip when they climb and to pull things to them.

Excessive Vocalization

Angora cats are not known for meowing too much, although they will "talk" to you at times. They seek attention by butting your hand or rubbing against your leg, but they will chirp in excitement or purr in contentment when they are snuggling with you. However, some people do have cats that loudly cry or meow and if your Angora cat does this, it could be cause for concern.

Excessive vocalization can be a sign of a physical or an emotional issue, although it is normal behavior for some cat breeds or individual cats. As cats age, they may "howl" at night as if they are lost and it can be caused when cats are going deaf or by senility in some senior cats. If your Angora cat starts loudly meowing, especially at night, call your vet to have him or her evaluated.

Chapter Six: Training and Behavior Modification

Aggressiveness

Even the most mild-mannered cat can turn aggressive in certain situations and people unwittingly encourage their aggression by giving into them when they are hissed or swatted. Aggression can be brought on by physical discomfort, illness or sometimes a situation will trigger aggression in a cat.

If they are in pain, if they are resting and don't wish to be bothered, if they are protecting their territory or offspring or when forced into prolonged eye contact, they can turn aggressive.

Some health problems like hyperthyroidism or hyperesthesia syndrome, which is a neurological disorder that can cause seizures, can cause them to become aggressive. If you haven't added a new cat to your household, if they are not protecting themselves or their territory and they turn aggressive, contact your veterinarian to have your cat evaluated for medical conditions that could be causing the problem.

Jumping Where They Shouldn't

Most Angora cats like to climb up as high as they can or jump up on high perches to hang out and relax, but there are places you may not want your cat to be.

If they jump on your kitchen counters, the top of a curio cabinet or up into your pantry, they could make a mess

Chapter Six: Training and Behavior Modification

by knocking over valuables or get into food they shouldn't be eating. There are many ways to discourage this behavior and teach them not to go where they are not wanted.

If a simple and firm "no!" doesn't work, consider squirting them with a small amount of water or using sticky paper in the places they like to perch to discourage them. Most cats do not like water and they will not appreciate having sticky paper on their paws. Aluminum foil is a good option if you don't wish to use sticky paper. This should help discourage them from jumping where you don't want them to be.

Before trying other options, first eliminate medical causes for your cat's bad behavior if he or she suddenly develops any of these issues. If your Angora cat starts behaving out of character, make an appointment with your vet to have them examined.

Catching a medical condition early will allow your cat to be treated and fully recover from any health problems they may have developed. Along with medical conditions, sometimes a cat's misbehaviors are caused by depression or other psychological issues and your vet should be able to diagnose and treat those problems as well.

Traveling with Your Cat

Traveling with a cat can be challenging, especially if you are driving in a vehicle. Most cats are not fond of being

Chapter Six: Training and Behavior Modification

in a moving vehicle, unless they have been taught to get used to it from a young age or they are an extraordinary cat.

Even though you may try to acclimate your cat to riding in a car when they are young, some cats never get used to it and do not enjoy the experience.

Unless your Angora cat has been trained to ride in a car, and likes the experience, you should always put your cat in a sturdy cat carrier when you go to the vet or on a trip. While you can use a soft-sided carrier, they are really made for airplane travel and it is better to use a hard-sided carrier when you're in a car.

The sturdier carrier gives them a bit more room to move around, especially as they are a bigger breed of cat, but it can also help protect your cat in case of an accident.

If you are traveling a short distance, such as to the vet, you may not need to make any extra preparations for your cat. However, if you are taking them on a longer trip, you will need to take some cat essentials along.

Traveling with a pet is much like traveling with a child, you need to take some supplies in order to make the trip more comfortable for them by keeping them calm.

Line their carrier with a blanket or a towel to give them something soft to cuddle up in, especially if you are traveling during the cooler months. An Angora cat can easily withstand cold weather, but they would still like to have something soft on which to lie.

Chapter Six: Training and Behavior Modification

Take water, food, bowls, a litter pan and litter on the trip to accommodate their needs. Place their favorite small toys in the carrier with them for both comfort and to give them something to pass the time.

The best place to put the carrier is in the middle of the back seat. This placement will prevent the sun from shining directly onto the carrier, which can make the trip uncomfortably warm for your Angora cat.

Secure the carrier with a seatbelt to keep it from sliding around on the seat in case you have to make a sudden stop or swerve the car. If the carrier isn't secure, your cat can be injured if the carrier overturns.

Some cats have motion sickness and it can be worsened if they can see outside during the trip. To help prevent their motion sickness, place their carrier on the floorboard behind one of the front seats. Try to prevent the floor air blower from directly blowing onto the carrier, especially if you have the heater on because it can get too hot for a thick furred Angora cat.

On a longer trip, you should set up a litter box inside of your vehicle. A covered litter pan works best because it will prevent the litter from spilling onto the floor of your vehicle.

Unlike dogs, your cat doesn't need to stretch its legs on a trip until you stop for the night. It is important that you keep your cat in its carrier while traveling, especially when

Chapter Six: Training and Behavior Modification

you stop so that it doesn't bolt out of the car and get lost in unfamiliar territory.

Traveling on an airplane has its own unique issues for you and your pet. Before you take them with you on a plane, you need to contact the airline to find out their pet policy before purchasing a ticket. Although it is faster to look for their policy on their website, policies are subject to change and you may wish to contact them directly to confirm the information on their site. Most airlines allow pets to be carried on the plane, which is what you should do with your cat.

A soft-sided pet carrier will fit under the seat in front of you, but you can also buy the seat beside you and place a hard-sided carrier on it. As you would when traveling by car, take some things with you to help comfort them. Place a blanket and their favorite toy in the carrier with them so they can snuggle while traveling.

You will need to get a health certificate from your cat's vet before traveling by plane. The airline will want to see that your cat has been vaccinated before you can take it on the plane. Keep the health certificate with you at all times so it is easily accessible. Put a collar on your cat with an identification tag with his or her name, your telephone number and address in case your cat manages to escape the carrier.

If you are traveling internationally on vacation, it would be better to have a trusted friend or family member

Chapter Six: Training and Behavior Modification

look after your cat while you're away than it would be to try to take your cat with you.

Unless you are moving to another country, making arrangements for a pet can be a hassle on short international trips. Some countries will not allow foreign animals into their country, while other countries require them to be quarantined on arrival. It can take weeks, if not months, to get approval to take your pet into another country.

Some cats may require a visit to their vet before you take your trip. Some of them need to be sedated because they do not travel well due to car or air-sickness. Always check with your veterinarian before giving your cat anything to keep it calm.

Some sedatives or tranquilizers will affect cat's body temperature or they may have other adverse reactions to them, even if they are made from natural herbs. It is better to let your vet sedate them or advise you on which sedative is best for your cat.

By being properly prepared and by taking the supplies your cat needs along on the trip, you can enjoy traveling with your cat. Work with your Angora cat to train them to lie calmly in a carrier so they will be used to it when it is time to take them on a trip. Start with small car rides across town and gradually make them longer so your cat will get used to car travel. They may never like it, but with patience and preparation, the travel experience will be better for you and your cat.

Chapter Six: Training and Behavior Modification

Chapter Seven: Vet Care for Your Angora Cat

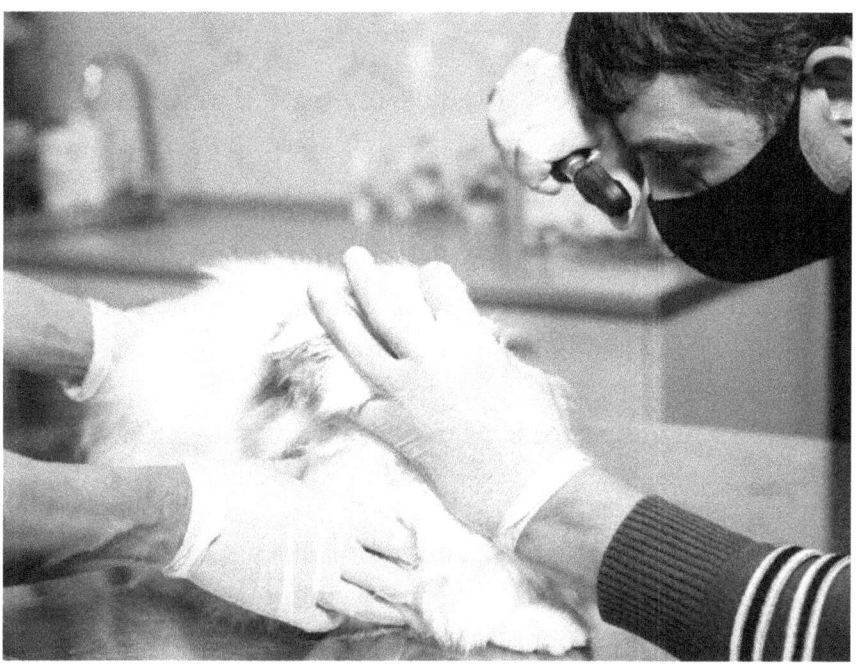

Getting an Angora cat is fun and exciting and you're probably eager to bring your new furry friend home, introduce her to the family, and play with her, but first you need to take a survey of that oh-so-necessary boring thing that is key to your Angora cat's happiness and longevity: health. This chapter will break down everything you need to do to ensure that your cat is healthy and will remain so.

Chapter Seven: Vet Care for Your Angora Cat

Vaccinations

If you're getting your Angora cat from a shelter, there's a very good chance that her shots are all up to date, but always check the paperwork provided to you and ask the professional staff there. If your Angora cat is coming from a pet store or a farm, there's a good chance that you'll need to vaccinate your pet.

Vaccinations are important, because they will help your Angora cat's immune system fight off some potentially fatal sicknesses. Not all vaccinations are necessary for all cats. Things like age and environment will determine which vaccines are necessary. Discuss which vaccines are necessary with your vet.

Most vets will recommend that all cats have at least the core vaccinations. These include vaccines for feline distemper, feline calici virus, feline herpes virus type 1, and rabies. Depending on whether a cat lives indoors or outdoors, the following vaccines may be necessary: feline leukemia virus, Bordetella, Chylamydophila felis, and feline immunodeficiency virus (ASPCA).

Flea and Tick Medication

Fleas and ticks are those gross little creatures that didn't receive an invitation to your house party, but beyond being a nuisance, they often carry diseases and cause anemia and excessive blood loss in your cat that could lead to death.

Chapter Seven: Vet Care for Your Angora Cat

The good news is that there are preventative medicines you can give to your cat to keep fleas and ticks from making a home in your cat's fur.

A few of the reputable medicines include Frontline, Advantage, and Revolution, which you dab or spray on every month. Talk to your vet about your best options for keeping the fleas and ticks off.

Vitamins

The necessity of daily vitamins for cats is as hotly debated as it is for humans. Do vitamins actually increase energy levels and overall health or are they a placebo designed to coax us out of our hard-earned dollars? Vitamins are a billion-dollar industry that anyone with the skill to set up a website and advertise a potion can take part in.

So how can we tell which are legitimately beneficial and which are kibbles crushed up in a capsule? The easy answer to that question is to talk with your vet before you purchase anything. The vet will be able to tell you if your cat has a certain vitamin deficiency and recommend vitamins that will actually serve the function they claim to.

The simple fact of the matter is that there's no sense spending money on vitamins if the vet checks your cat out and tells you that she is perfectly healthy on her current diet.

Chapter Seven: Vet Care for Your Angora Cat

Spaying and Neutering

Spaying or neutering are beneficial for a variety of reasons. Spaying is the removal of the ovaries and uterus of a female cat, and neutering is the removal of the testicles from a male cat. Besides preventing the surprise production of kittens, these procedures serve to increase your cat's lifespan, improve his behavior, and increase overall health. Chances of getting some forms of cancer are significantly diminished in spayed and neutered cats.

The surgeries are routine procedures that take little time and almost always result in a speedy recovery. A cat will experience discomfort but shouldn't be in pain after surgery. To aid recovery, keep her from running and jumping for a few days. Distract her from licking the incision site by giving her treats or having her wear a cone. Consider using shredded paper in place of litter to keep the incision site from getting dust stuck in it. Your cat should be healed within ten days. If you notice any unusual swelling or redness, consult your vet.

An Angora cat can undergo the spaying or neutering procedure as young as eight-week-old. If your cat is older, it's still likely that your cat can be spayed or neutered. Talk with your vet about when the best time is to do this. Usually, it's best not to do it when the cat is in heat, as this can cause increased blood loss during the surgery.

Chapter Seven: Vet Care for Your Angora Cat

To Declaw or Not to Declaw?

It's hotly debated whether indoor cats ought to be declawed. The pros are that the cat won't be able to ruin things with scratching or scratch other family members. Experts recommend using this as a last resort when the only other option is getting rid of kitty.

The cons are far more extensive. Declawing consists of the amputation of the cat's third knuckle, which is typically painful for the cat and can result in arthritis and other permanent future conditions. A declawed cat might develop an aversion to having his feet touched and experience diminished agility. A cat who spends time outdoors should never be declawed, as removing the claws leaves him defenseless against wild animals that could hurt him.

Alternatives include trimming of the claws, tenectomy, which is the cutting of the tendons that extend the claws (some argue that this is just as bad as declawing, however), and training the cat to use a scratching post—instead of your pretty wood banister.

Exercise

Angora cats have an exceptionally high metabolism, but they still require exercise to keep them from sloth and obesity. Playing with your cat a few times every day will help keep her muscles toned and stave off cathood obesity, heart disease, and diabetes. A sedentary lifestyle isn't good for anyone, including your cat.

Signs of Illness

Diseases do not develop overnight. It takes time before your Angora cat falls ill. You need to be able to notice when your cat starts to show abnormal behavior even before it falls ill. You can only do this having interacted and socialized with your cat to a point where you can easily tell when it is about to fall ill. Signs of illness in cats can be categorized into two categories; behavioral and physical signs.

Behavioral Signs

You should be able to notice different unusual behavior by your Angora cat, behavior that should prompt you to take your cat to a vet at the earliest possible opportunity unless you know the reason for any unusual behavior.

Although your cat will avoid its litter box when the box is unclean, avoidance of the same is usually a clear sign of a medical condition. Urination outside the litter box can be a sign of such medical conditions as diabetes, urinary tract infection or kidney failure. You need to take your cat to a vet in case you notice this unusual behavior more than once when the litter box is perfectly clean.

Chapter Seven: Vet Care for Your Angora Cat

Angora cats generally are not fond of drinking water. They obtain the water they need from their food. Although your cat will occasionally drink water, increased intake of water should be a cause of concern. This will be a sign of thirst, which is usually a sign of health conditions/diseases such as diabetes and hyperthyroidism, among other diseases.

Failure by your Angora cat to eat as it normally does should be a serious cause of concern. This may be an indication of loss of appetite that may in turn be a sign of many diseases including gingivitis, trauma or anemia among many other diseases.

Interacting and socializing with your cat should make it possible for you to know when and why it meows. Excess meowing (vocalization) may be a sign of stress, fear, sickness, pain or another medical condition.

Your Angora cat is most likely to spend a better part of the day and in particular during the morning hours sleeping. Although this is perfectly normal, excessive sleep in addition to hiding when it is awake should be a sign of fear, anxiety or sickness.

Being people-oriented, your Angora cat will most likely get into the habit of welcoming you whenever you arrive at home. You will need to be concerned with any change in this habit. You will need to establish where your cat goes when not welcoming you. It is most likely that you will find your cat in its litter box, which should alert you of a medical problem.

Chapter Seven: Vet Care for Your Angora Cat

Physical Signs

Unlike behavioral signs of sickness, physical signs are easy to notice and one of the most obvious signs you should be able to notice is a change in your cat's coat appearance. The fact that cats generally groom themselves means that your cat's coat should always be smooth. You should be concerned when the coat appears ruffled, which may be a sign of malnutrition, parasitic infection or such other skin disorders as ringworm or allergy.

Your cat should always have good breath. Bad breath will definitely not be normal since such may be a sign of diabetes, gingivitis, kidney disease or gastrointestinal disorder among other diseases/health conditions.

Any rapid weight loss or gain should be a serious concern. This is so because such may be a sign of many health conditions including malnutrition, overfeeding, diabetes, kidney failure or heart disease among many others.

Regardless of your Angora cat's age, five very important factors determine how healthy it will be; proper nutrition and weight management, environment, good dental care, parasite control and vaccinations. The food that you feed your cat on determines whether or not it will remain healthy throughout its lifetime. You also need to make your cat's environment as friendly as possible to allow it to enjoy its life to the fullest. Ensure that you do not only socialize with your cat but engage in play activities as well.

Chapter Seven: Vet Care for Your Angora Cat

Ensuring that your cat's oral health is at its optimum will also go a long way in preventing many diseases. Closely related to environment is the issue of parasites. Note that parasites thrive in unhygienic locations and it is therefore very necessary to ensure that your cat's room or space remains clean all the time. Lastly, you need to ensure that your cat receives all the recommended vaccinations and any other vaccination that may be fronted by relevant authorities from time to time.

When to Visit a Vet

When to take your cat to a vet depends on its age. Although kittens are in most cases sold off when they have already received the most important vaccinations, you will need to take yours to a vet at least three times in a year for any additional vaccinations or routine checkups. Doing so will make it possible for you to know any health issues that your kitten may have once it comes of age.

An adult Angora cat does not require too much vet attention so long as you feed it on recommended foods and keep its environment clean. Your adult cat will have received the recommended vaccinations and should be in a position to remain healthy for a long time. You will need to take it to a vet at least twice in a year for routine checkups.

Having an old or aging cat can be a little bit of a problem because of the many visits you may need to make to a vet clinic. This is because it is during old age that such age-

Chapter Seven: Vet Care for Your Angora Cat

related diseases/health conditions as arthritis and heart disease, among others, set in. You will need to take your aging cat to a vet at least three times in a year for routine medical checkups and for such indicated diseases/health conditions.

Your cat's general health remains squarely in your hands. You should take every step possible to ensure that your cat is not at risk of contracting any disease. You should be in a position to perform at-home physical examinations on a regular basis with the aim of determining your cat's general health condition.

Although you need to take your kitten, cat or aging cat to a vet as indicated, there are instances when it becomes necessary to take it to a vet at the earliest opportunity possible. Such incidents as accidents require that you take your cat to a vet for immediate medical attention.

The Veterinarian

The professionals commonly referred to as veterinarians or vets in short are actually veterinary physicians trained to treat diseases, disorders and injuries that affect non-human animals. Vets are referred to differently in different countries around the world. Although they are generally referred to as vets, they are professionally referred to as veterinary surgeons in the UK for instance.

Different countries have strict legislations when it comes to veterinary services, just the same way it is with

Chapter Seven: Vet Care for Your Angora Cat

human physicians. It is mandatory in almost all countries for anyone using the term 'vet' to have undertaken the necessary training, registered and license to practice as a vet. Vets work in many institutions. There are those who work in vet clinics where they engage with animal owners or pet owners directly in treating their livestock. There are also those who work in such institutions as zoos, research institutions and animal hospitals.

Just in the same way that human doctors specialize in a specific area, vets also specialize. You are therefore most likely to come across a vet who is a surgery or dermatology specialist or one specializing in internal medicine. Generally, vets diagnose and treat non-human diseases and health conditions in addition to providing aftercare and administration of vaccines.

It is common practice to find vets in different countries working in the private sector. Only a small number work in government institutions. The fact that the majority work in private sectors and in particular in clinics allows them to work directly with animal owners, owners whose animals have varied diseases and health conditions. The fact that you plan to buy or already own a cat and an Angora cat for that matter will obviously make it necessary to pay a vet a visit. This can be on the first day when you bring the cat home for the requisite vaccine(s). Just like with choosing your personal physician, you need to carefully choose a vet to engage for your cat's treatment and administration of vaccines.

Chapter Seven: Vet Care for Your Angora Cat

How to Find a Good Vet

The fact that most vets work in clinics and private clinics makes finding the best vet a big challenge. This can be very true if you live in a location where there are many practicing vets. The first way to finding the right vet is to enquire from close family members, neighbors and friends with pets. They should be able to refer you to a vet they personally know and who provides quality service.

Apart from making enquiries, you also have the option of consulting your local professional organization for information on licensed vets practicing in your locality. You also have the option of getting information on the right vets from a local cat breeder. A breeder in particular will be better placed to refer you to the right vet because he/she obviously engages the service of a vet to treat his/her cats in the cattery.

Whether you choose to make enquiries or contact a professional organization or a cat breeder, there are certainly several issues you will need to ascertain before you engage the service of a vet and one of these issues is whether or not the vet is licensed and enjoys some accreditation. A professional and ethical vet will normally share with you his certification, which should ideally be posted on the office wall. You will also need to ascertain whether or not the vet is a member of a local professional organization.

Apart from a vet's certification, accreditation and level of experience, you need to undertake an overall assessment of the facility with knowledge that it is at that clinic where you will hence forth be bringing your Angora cat in case of health

Chapter Seven: Vet Care for Your Angora Cat

problems. It is therefore important to assess a facility's level of cleanliness among other issues.

It is common for vets to enter into agreements with pet owners for the purpose of taking care of their pets' health. Although most pet owners are in favor of such agreements as one way of cutting down on their pets' health care costs, doing so can be costly without due diligence.

It is possible that you and your pet's vet can have disagreements that force you to engage the service of a different vet. Terminating an agreement can be very costly depending on the period you agreed upon. The best way to cut down on your cat's health care costs is to shop for a suitable pet insurance policy that covers risks that your cat is susceptible to.

Cat Insurance

Your Angora cat is not only people-friendly; it turns out to be the best companion you can have at home as a pet. Furthermore, it makes you active because of its playful nature. It is definitely a valuable family member. Just in the same way that you ensure your other family members are comfortable and in good health, you need to ensure that your cat also remains in good health and one way to go about this is to take out cat insurance for your Angora.

It is a fact that veterinary fees and medication costs are always on the rise, which can make it impossible for you to

Chapter Seven: Vet Care for Your Angora Cat

meet your cat's medical costs at a time it needs it most. Taking out an appropriate cat insurance policy goes a long way in keeping your veterinary costs low while giving your cat good health care.

Regardless of your location, any cat insurance policy you are likely to find is designed to cover the cost of veterinary fees and treatment of diseases/health conditions and injuries. Although very important, choosing the right cat insurance policy for your cat can be a big challenge. This is because there are simply many policies out there in the market that differ in terms of what they cover and price. This makes it necessary to know the best time to take out cat insurance.

The best time to take out cat insurance is when your cat is young, a kitten. This is because age is one of the most important factors pet insurance companies take into consideration when determining the level of insurance premium to quote. Kittens generally attract low premium rates compared to adult and aging cats that attract high premium rates because of various factors including onset of age-related diseases/health conditions.

There are generally four types of cat insurance policies you can choose from; lifetime, maximum benefit, limited time and accident-only policies.

Lifetime cat insurance policy covers vet fees for one year. You will need to continuously renew the policy to enjoy the same cover at the same premium rate regardless of how many claims you make. Although the cost of this policy is

Chapter Seven: Vet Care for Your Angora Cat

usually on the higher side, it is beneficial taking into account the fact that your cat remains covered for its lifetime even when it develops life-long disease.

Unlike the lifetime policy, the maximum benefit policy provides cover for a pre-determined maximum amount of veterinary fees per health condition. The specific health condition is considered a pre-existing condition and is therefore excluded from future claims once the maximum limit is reached.

The time limited policy is similar to the maximum benefit policy except that the latter is limited to one year only, a period in which vet fees can be offset for each health condition.

The accident-only policy is limited to treatment of injuries your cat may sustain from accidents at home or outside the home including on the road.

A common feature of almost all cat insurance policies is the exclusion of pre-existing medical conditions. Such other procedures as preventative treatments, pregnancy/birth, neutering/spaying and worm control are also excluded from the policies. It is very important that you undertake some little research with the aim of finding a pet insurance company that quotes low premium rates on policies that provide a specific cover you need for your Angora cat.

Chapter Seven: Vet Care for Your Angora Cat

Common Feline Diseases

The fact that Angora cats are not prone to many diseases and health conditions does not mean that they are not susceptible to other feline diseases that other breeds of cats suffer from. Allowing your Angora cat to roam widely exposes it to a good number of diseases. Some of these include:

Hypertrophic Cardiomyopathy (HCM)

This is the most serious hereditary disease that affects most cat breeds, including the Angora breed. The disease causes stiffening of the heart wall, in effect restricting flow of blood. This can lead to instant heart failure. Although the disease presents no symptoms, such symptoms as lethargy, excessive weight loss, labored breathing, excessive heart murmur and lameness on rear legs should be a cause of concern.

It is important that you take your cat to a vet immediately you notice any of these symptoms for proper check up, diagnosis and treatment.

Inflammatory Bowel Disease (IBD)

IBD is a term used to refer to several diseases and health conditions that affect a cat's gastrointestinal tract and whose cause(s) remain largely unknown. One characteristic

Chapter Seven: Vet Care for Your Angora Cat

of all the diseases is that they cause inflammation of the intestines.

Your Angora cat will present several symptoms if affected. Some of these include diarrhea, signs of depression, flatulence, abdominal pain, general body weakness, bloody stool and distressed hair on the coat.

Diagnosis of IBD is normally through laboratory tests including blood count, biochemistry profile and urinalysis. Although cure for IBD is not available, a vet will normally institute control measures that include stabilization of body weight, reduction of immune system response and administration of antibiotic medications.

Upper Respiratory Infection

This is a disease that mainly affects kittens. However, the kittens do overcome the disease as they grow. The disease presents such symptoms as sniffing, runny eyes and coughing among other symptoms. Upper respiratory infection is caused by two viruses; Calicivirus and Rhinotracheitis virus. These two viruses attack the lining of the upper respiratory tract and spreads very fast among kittens since it is transmitted through sneezing.

Familial Amyloidosis

This is not a disease but rather a health condition that affects the liver. It is actually a group of disorders with similar characteristic; abnormal deposition of Amyloid (a fibrous protein) into body tissues. Amyloid occurs as a hard and waxy substance and develops as a result of degeneration of tissue. The disposition interferes with the normal functioning of areas where the protein has reached. Familial Amyloidosis is a hereditary health disorder common in Abyssinians, Nebelungs, Burmese and Turkish Angora breed of cats.

Although this is a hereditary disorder, it can also be caused by various factors including chronic infection, inflammation of inner layer of the heart caused by bacterial endocarditis and tumour. The condition presents several symptoms including general body weakness, loss of appetite, excessive thirst and urination, vomiting, enlarged abdomen and swelling of the limbs accompanied by joint pain.

Familial Amyloidosis is not treatable. It is a disorder that impairs the liver, seriously affecting its function and that of other body organs and most cats die from the disease. There are however specific measures that your vet can take to lessen the pain and help prolong your cat's life in case of infection. Your vet may take such measures as blood transfusion (blood change), fluid therapy, diet change and in some cases surgery.

Gingivitis

Chapter Seven: Vet Care for Your Angora Cat

Gingivitis is a periodontal disease. It causes inflammation of the gums that turn reddish. Plaque formation also occurs. Plaque is basically a collection of debris, food, dead skin, mucous and bacteria. The gingival surface however remains very smooth. The disease can easily be reversed at the earliest stage through proper dental care.

Without proper dental care, the disease develops further with occurrence of calculus under the gums. Calculus is a mixture of organic matter, carbonate and calcium phosphate. In addition to further development of plaque, the gum surface becomes irregular with some pain in the gums.

As the disease progresses, it forms a narrow space between the teeth and the inner wall of the gum. The bacteria present in this space mutate and release toxins that damage gingival tissue. Occurrence of gingivitis is common not only in cats but also in dogs aged three years and above.

Apart from the swelling and reddishness of the gums, other symptoms of the disease include bad breath. Gingivitis is largely caused by accumulation of plaque. There are also other risk factors that encourage occurrence of the disease. These include excessive soft food, old age, bad chewing habits, diabetes, breathing through the mouth, crowded teeth and autoimmune disease among other risk factors.

Because of the danger that gingivitis poses to your cat, you need to help your cat in preventing occurrence of the disease. This you can do by ensuring that your cat's oral health remains at its optimum by brushing its teeth at least twice in a week with veterinarian toothpaste or using a finger

Chapter Seven: Vet Care for Your Angora Cat

pad to clean the teeth. This simple action goes a long way in preventing build-up of plaque.

A serious case of gingivitis requires veterinarian attention at the earliest possible time. In addition to physical examination, your vet will, as a matter of routine, try to establish possible causes of the disease, which can be the kind of food you feed your cat on.

There are several ways through which your vet may choose to treat the disease, depending on his/her findings. Your vet may prescribe antibacterial solution for squirting on your cat's teeth to prevent build-up of plaque, prescribe dietary supplements or prescribe specific foods that help in promoting good dental health.

In case of serious gingivitis, your vet may choose to remove baby (deciduous) teeth that may cause teeth overcrowding, which is a cause of the disease or remove particular affected teeth. It is also possible that your vet may choose to only remove plaque and calculus before polishing teeth surface.

Gingivitis is a serious gum disease that you must not let your cat suffer from. This is so because it reaches a stage where your cat will not be able to chew food properly or even eat due to pain. You will certainly not rule out malnourishment and possible death of your pet.

Pyruvate Kinase Deficiency

Chapter Seven: Vet Care for Your Angora Cat

Pyruvate Kinase is an enzyme which deficiency in your cat's body leads to impairment of red blood cells, greatly reducing the ability of red blood cells to metabolize. The inability of red blood cells to metabolize causes anemia in addition to other blood issues. Pyruvate Kinase deficiency is also very common in such breed of cats as the Nebelung, Tonkinese, Abyssinian and other short-haired cat breeds.

Caused by defects in genes acquired at birth, Pyruvate Kinase deficiency presents such symptoms as body weakness, anaemia, jaundice and increased heart rate among other symptoms. This condition is usually addressed through bone marrow transplant, which is the only treatment method available. In addition to being an expensive treatment, it is also life-threatening. Most cats that suffer from this condition die by the time they attain four years.

Spinal Muscular Atrophy (SMA)

This is another hereditary disease that all breed of cats remain susceptible to. It affects kittens in most cases. While an affected kitten remains normal in other areas of the body, the rear legs show signs of lameness. This is because the disease impairs neurons found within the spinal cord. Reputable Angora cat breeders do engage vets to carry out tests on their kittens to ascertain presence of the disease before the kittens are sold off.

Hyperthyroidism

Chapter Seven: Vet Care for Your Angora Cat

This is an endocrine disorder whose occurrence is directly linked to over-activity of the thyroid gland, which leads to excess levels of specific hormones. These hormones play a very important role in the body; the role of controlling metabolism. Increased levels of these hormones have the negative effect of increasing your cat's heart rate with the possibility of your cat developing heart murmur. Without appropriate treatment, the disease easily causes heart failure, kidney damage, high blood pressure and death.

Your cat will exhibit a number of symptoms when infected. These include diarrhoea, vomiting, behavioural changes, weight loss, increased thirst and urination, body weakness, poor coat condition and rapid heartbeat among other symptoms. These symptoms may not necessarily point at hyperthyroidism because the same symptoms are presented by other cat diseases, including cat diabetes and renal failure. It is therefore very important that you take your cat to a vet once you notice any of these symptoms.

The fact that hyperthyroidism does not affect specific breeds of cats means that all cats are at risk of suffering from the disease. It mostly affects older cats and dogs. There are two main ways of treating hyperthyroidism. A treatment method a vet chooses depends on your cat's medical condition.

Your vet may choose to prescribe such medications as Tapazole, whose action is not to treat but to control the disease. Your cat will need to use prescribed medication(s) for the rest of its life. There are instances when a vet may choose to undertake surgery with the aim of removing the enlarged

Chapter Seven: Vet Care for Your Angora Cat

thyroid. The other treatment your vet may choose is to implement radioactive iodine treatment, which involves injection of a single dose of radioactive iodine. Iodine has the positive effect of destroying the damaged part of the thyroid while leaving normal thyroid tissues intact.

Kidney Disease

Kidney disease is one disease that is often ignored when looking at cat diseases. All cats regardless of breed are susceptible to kidney disease. The kidney plays the important role of removing waste from the bloodstream in addition to regulating the amount of fluids in the body. Failure by the kidneys to play these vital roles puts a cat's life in serious danger.

Kidney disease presents different symptoms including loss of appetite, frequent vomiting, depression, poor coat appearance and frequent urination or no urination. Kidney disease can be acute or sudden and chronic or long-term. It can be caused by such factors as trauma, surgery, shock, serious blood loss, poison, drugs and infection of the kidneys.

Unlike other cat diseases that present symptoms almost immediately, symptoms associated with kidney disease only appear when a large part of the kidneys is already destroyed. It is therefore very necessary that you take your cat for regular veterinary checkups.

Chapter Seven: Vet Care for Your Angora Cat

Retinol Atrophy

Retinal atrophy is a non-treatable hereditary disease common in some cat breeds. The disease is also common in some dog breeds. It is the degeneration of retina, causing gradual loss of vision, which ends in blindness. The disease presents such symptoms as decreased vision at night, dilated pupils and cataract formation among other symptoms.

Arthritis

Arthritis refers to negative changes that occur within joints. These changes develop when cartilage that protects different bone joints wear out, causing friction at the joints. The friction causes swelling accompanied by pain. Although the cartilage is supposed to be replaced naturally, arthritis is bound to occur when it wears out faster than it is replaced.

Just like in humans, onset of arthritis in cats is in advanced age although middle aged cats can also suffer from the condition. The swelling and accompanying pain is usually chronic, which causes a lot of discomfort.

There is no cure for Arthritis. It can only be treated with any treatment that a vet offers, treatment that aims at lessening the pain and swelling that your cat experiences. Treatment needs to be offered at the earliest possible time so as to prevent further loss of cartilage.

Although arthritis is common in such other cat breeds as the Himalayan, Siamese and Persian cat breeds, your

Chapter Seven: Vet Care for Your Angora Cat

Angora cat can suffer from the condition due to such factors as old age, obesity, congenital defects, accidents and infection.

Arthritis has a serious effect on a cat's health. This is because it does not only make a cat uncomfortable but impairs its mobility as well. The condition presents such symptoms as limited activity, stiffness in walking, limping and social withdrawal.

Although your vet will definitely prescribe medications that help in preventing swelling and managing pain, he/she is likely to recommend the most appropriate diet for your cat as the most effective treatment option. This is because food plays a very important role in your cat's overall health.

Allergic Dermatitis

Allergic dermatitis refers to conditions that affect the skin negatively. These can be caused by such factors as food allergy, parasites, hormonal imbalances and infections. One effective way to prevent allergic dermatitis in your cat is to feed it on food rich in meat-based protein, essential fatty acids and antioxidants.

There are instances when you may need to take your cat to a vet. This is when the skin is not only rough but has wounds. Your cat's skin should be smooth and soft without any signs of flakes. Hair on the skin should also be evenly spread out.

Chapter Seven: Vet Care for Your Angora Cat

Diabetes

Just like in humans, cats suffer from diabetes when their metabolic system cannot effectively control the amount of sugar in their blood stream. The main cause of this is usually lack of or limited production of insulin, which is produced in the pancreas. Apart from insufficient amount of insulin, your cat is at risk of developing diabetes in case it is obese, approaching old age, is a male, stressed, poor diet and hormonal imbalances.

Diabetes presents several symptoms including excessive thirst, rapid weight loss, loss of appetite, vomiting, increased urination and general body weakness among other symptoms.

Once diagnosed, your vet may recommend a number of ways to help your cat cope. One of the most effective ways your vet is most likely to recommend is diet, the kind of food you feed your cat on. A vegetarian diet with proper nutrient profile is usually very effective in managing diabetes in cats.

Gastrointestinal Disorders

These disorders also include disorders of a cat's digestive system. These are disorders that hinder smooth digestion and absorption of nutrients contained in the food that your cat eats. Gastrointestinal disorders in particular interfere with both the intestine and stomach causing pain and, in some cases, swelling. Some of these disorders include

Chapter Seven: Vet Care for Your Angora Cat

acute gastroenteritis, colitis, diarrhea, constipation, irritable bowel syndrome and pancreatitis among others.

Occurrence of these disorders presents several symptoms including vomiting, flatulence, body weakness, constipation, diarrhea and in some cases regurgitation.

Although they do not present any immediate danger, gastrointestinal and digestive disorders can become life-threatening if not addressed in good time. You need to take your cat to a vet for correct diagnosis and treatment. Treatment options available do aim at alleviating the pain and suffering that your cat experiences in addition to eliminating symptoms. One of the most effective treatment options available relates to the food that you feed your cat on. Vets do recommend highly digestible foods for cats with these conditions. Other recommended food types include high soluble foods.

You will be obligated to prevent occurrence of these disorders for the benefit of your cat. This will mean ascertaining specific factors or food stuffs that may be the cause of such disorders.

Heart Disease

Your Angora cat is at risk of suffering from heart disease and like with most cat diseases, the food you feed your cat on plays a major role in preventing or encouraging the disease. There are however other factors that may cause

Chapter Seven: Vet Care for Your Angora Cat

heart disease in your cat including old age and heartworm among other factors.

Heart disease has the negative effect of enlarging your cat's heart, making it inefficient. In effect, the heart holds more fluid than it is supposed to hold. A clever way to go about preventing excessive fluid in your cat's heart is to feed it cat food low on sodium.

Heart disease presents several symptoms some similar to those presented by other cat diseases. These include low-pitched cough, difficulty in breathing, weight gain/loss and abdominal swelling among other symptoms.

Urinary Tract Infections

UTIs are various infections that do affect both the bladder and urethra. Of the infections, feline idiopathic cystitis (FIC) is the most prevalent. Thought to be caused by excessive level of stress, it causes inflammation of the urinary tract in addition to forming crystals along a cat's urinary tract. Such crystals are in most cases those of calcium oxalate.

UTIs present different symptoms including inappropriate urination, straining during urination, loss of bladder control, colored urine, licking of the genitals, loss of appetite and lack of interest in any activity among other symptoms.

UTIs can be caused by several factors including obesity, diet composed of foods rich in magnesium, calcium, phosphorous and protein (unbalanced), surgery and infections. Any UTI can be very problematic since occurrence rate remains high after treatment. This becomes real when the causative factor is not addressed before treatment is offered. Vets emphasize on the need to feed your cat on the right cat food that is not only nutritious but also well balanced.

Obesity

Acquisition of food in the wild for any creature, including cats, is not an easy task. Cats in the wild have to literally hunt and chase after their prey to feed on. The physical exertion definitely takes a toll on their bodies and it is therefore not easy to find an obese cat in the wild. Things are different for domesticated cats including Angora cats. Domesticated cats have it very easy when it comes to food simply because all that they eat is readily provided, which poses the risk of obesity.

From the study findings of a research study conducted by Association for Pet Obesity Prevention (APOP) in 2011, over 50% of cats in the USA were found to be either obese or overweight. It therefore simply means that your Angora cat is also at risk of becoming obese even though it is one of the most active cat breeds you can find.

Simply put, your cat is most likely to become obese when its energy intake is more that the amount of energy it requires. Just like in humans, its body converts the extra energy it consumes into fat, which gets deposited in specific

Chapter Seven: Vet Care for Your Angora Cat

locations within its body. Getting rid of deposited fat can be a big challenge, even with regulation of energy intake.

Living with an obese Angora cat or any obese cat for that matter can be very expensive. This is so because obesity forms the foundation of a wide range of diseases and health conditions that will see you in and out of a vet's clinic on a regular basis. Just like in humans, obesity in cats causes such diseases as arthritis, heart disease, diabetes, cancer of the bladder and breathing difficulty.

The ideal weight of your Angora cat should be between 7-10 pounds (3.5-5 kg) and between 5-8 pounds (2.5-4kg) for a male and female respectively. You need to take anything beyond these as a cause of concern. It is therefore important that you have your cat weighed whenever you call at the vet for regular checkups, which should ideally include weight measurement.

You should however be able to tell whether your cat is becoming obese or not even without weighing it. You should be able to feel your cat's backbone and ribs whenever you place your hand on its back. Failure to feel the bones should be a clear sign of obesity.

Obesity is a serious health condition in cats. Just like in humans, obesity in cats encourages occurrence of such serious diseases/health conditions as diabetes, heart disease and cardiovascular diseases. Ensuring that your Angora cat maintains normal body weight goes a long way in preventing regular trips to a vet's clinic, which translates to reduced health care costs.

Chapter Seven: Vet Care for Your Angora Cat

Your cat can become obese for several reasons, one of which is free feeding. Most cats left free to choose when to eat often develop obesity. This is so because a free feeding program gives a cat the opportunity to overeat, in effect consuming too much food that its body does not really need. Veterinarians recommend feeding your adult cat between two to three meals in a day with the amount of each meal controlled to avoid overeating. Ideally, your cat's food should be about half of a human meal.

The other main cause of obesity in cats is intake of too many calories. Unlike humans, your cat does not have the Amylase enzyme that digests carbohydrates contained in their food. The enzyme plays the very important role of breaking down large carbohydrate molecules into smaller absorbable units of glucose.

Furthermore, cats are not carbohydrate consumers by nature. Because most dry cat foods contain high levels of carbohydrates, you need to shop carefully for the same. Any dry cat food you buy should have minimal carbohydrates, if any. It is highly recommended that you feed your cat a diet that is similar to its natural food, which makes canned cat food stuffs better. A cat's ideal diet should be high on meat-based protein and moderate fat and water.

Apart from carbohydrates and a free feeding program, the other main cause of obesity in cats is cat treats. Availability of cat treats has made many cat owners lazy when it comes to feeding their cats. Many cat owners rely on cat treats as their cats' main food. Cat treats contain high levels of carbohydrates and feeding your cat on the same on

Chapter Seven: Vet Care for Your Angora Cat

a regular basis puts it at great risk of becoming obese. You should only feed your cat on treats at special occasions as a way of appreciation or reward.

Unlike in humans, obesity in cats is a non-hereditary health condition. Your cat will only develop obesity because of what you feed it on. It is therefore very necessary that you pay attention to what your cat eats and in what amounts.

Apart from food, you seriously need to ensure that your cat is physically engaged on a daily basis. Exercises are very important not only for your cat's physique but also in stimulating its mind. You need to make effective use of cat toys to help your cat burn excess fat deposits in the body.

Formulating a balanced and nutritious weight loss diet should also be effective in helping your cat cut down on excess body weight just in case it has already become obese. You need to formulate a diet that is low on carbohydrates but high on meat-based protein and other nutrients including fresh drinking water.

Pustule

Pustule in cats is what acne is to humans. Just like in humans who suffer acne mostly on the facial area, your cat is also likely to suffer acne that affects its chin although its lower lip can also be affected. Major causes of pustule in cats happen to be poor grooming (lack of it) and excess oil on the skin surface, oil produced from within the body.

Chapter Seven: Vet Care for Your Angora Cat

Just like acne in humans, your cat is most likely to present such symptoms as black/whiteheads, swollen chin and development of nodules that can be very painful. Your cat can end up having boils as a result of pustule.

A vet will normally try to rule out such health issues as feline leprosy, allergy and skin tumor before diagnosing pustule. Confirmation of correct diagnosis is usually through such procedures as fungal culture, biopsy test and skin scrapping among other procedures.

For treatment, a vet will normally prescribe antibiotics, topical creams and shampoos. Regular occurrence of pustules should be a cause of concern regarding your cat's general health. It may be necessary for a vet to undertake your cat's full health scan to ascertain the exact cause of the same.

Chapter Seven: Vet Care for Your Angora Cat

Chapter Eight: Showing Your Angora Cat

Preparing For Show

In order to prepare to show an Angora Cat in The International Cat Association (TICA), you should read the TICA show rules; look over the TICA show calendar for specific show dates; and you should go to the TICA website to print out a downloadable Checklist for your first cat show (The International Cat Association, 2012). To show an Angora Kitten, the Kitten must be at least 4 months old; and to show an Angora Adult Cat, the Adult must be at least 8 months old.

One important requirement to do before showing your Angora Cat is to make sure his/her rabies vaccine is current

Chapter Eight: Showing Your Angora Cat

and up to date. It is suggested to wait until a Cat is 6 months old before giving your Cat the rabies vaccine because of the side effects of that vaccine.

What Is The Description Of An Angora Cat To Show?

An Angora Cat to show at The International Cat Association is generally described as perfectly-balanced, graceful creature with a fine, silky coat. In judging, refinement is more important than size. This should especially be taken into consideration when comparing males to females.

How are Angora Cats judged in show?

Angora Cats are judges in show and can receive ribbons. Angora Cats are called up according to the Angora breed, division, and color/pattern. Judges will announce their best, second best, and third best of breed.

TICA Color and Division Award Ribbons are as follows:

Color	Place	Points	Division
Blue	1st	25	Black
Red	2nd	20	Purple

Chapter Eight: Showing Your Angora Cat

Yellow   3rd   15   Orange

The Angora Cat Pedigree

The Angora Cat pedigree shows your cat name and the family tree of your cat. It is needed when you want to enter your Angora Cat into a TICA cat show.

What To Prepare If You Want To Enter Your Angora into A Cat Show:

- Cage curtains.
- Kitty litter; a litter pan, water; and food dishes.
- A rug for the bottom of the cage.
- Nail clippers.
- Any necessary grooming equipment such as a brush.
- Confirmation slip received from the Entry Clerk.
- Vaccination records for your Angora Cat entry.
- Pedigree and Registration papers.

Chapter Eight: Showing Your Angora Cat

TICA Angora Cat Standard

For the Angora Cat Standard at TICA, cats are judged according to the following point system:

HEAD . . . . 40 points

Shape 9

Ears 12

Eyes 4

Chin 2

Muzzle 2

Nose 2

Profile 5

Neck 4

BODY . . . . 40 points

Torso 9

Legs/Feet 9

Tail 8

Boning 9

Musculature 5

COAT/COLOR . . . 15 points

Coat 10

Color 5

OTHER . . . 5 points

Balance 10

Chapter Eight: Showing Your Angora Cat

Chapter Nine: Breeding Your Angora Cat

Breeding your Angora cat is not an activity that one can take lightly; you should have a broad understanding of everything that will be involved in the process. It takes a lot of knowledge, dedication, time and deep pocket. This chapter will talk about the things you have to know when planning to breed your Angora cat.

Things To Remember When Breeding Your Angora Cat

1. **Pay attention to your cat.**

Chapter Nine: Breeding Your Angora Cat

You need to be able to tell when your cat is in heat. Don't just let your cat go. This is the first step so that you will know what to do next if you want your cat to produce offspring.

2. Be careful in the mating process for your cat.

Be wary of which tomcat your cat wants to mate as it may pick one that may not be the best choice.

3. Choose an owner that you can trust.

An owner of a male cat that you can trust will maximize the chances of your cat producing the best offspring.

Reproduction

The instinct of procreation is inherent in all living things. Of course, cats are no exception. However, there are notable differences between domestic and wild cats. A wild cat has a mating season once a year, and the number of cubs born by one female is less than that of a domestic cat, in which a surge of sexual activity occurs 2 times a year - in spring and in summer. The heat in a domestic cat continues for about weeks. If fertilization did not occur at this time, after a few weeks it repeats again.

The fertility of cats is well known to many of their owners. If the animal freely walks the streets, it can bring 2-3 litters per year. During estrus, the cat's behavior changes

Chapter Nine: Breeding Your Angora Cat

dramatically. An affectionate and calm animal becomes irritable, screams often and loudly, rolls on the floor, rubs against walls and door frames, and often refuses food. For these reasons sometimes it is thought that it is much easier to keep a cat than a cat. However, males also have some behavioral features that create certain difficulties for the owners. Like many other animals, they have developed an instinct to mark territory. The substance secreted by the anal glands of cats has a strong and persistent odor that lasts for a very long time. Therefore, if the owner does not intend use your pet for reproduction, it is advisable to expose it to castration. Healthy animals usually tolerate this operation easily. However, in order for the cat not to manifest the instinct of marking the territory, it should be carried out as early as possible. The cat can also be spayed if offspring are undesirable.

Some owners believe that it is inhumane to carry out such operations on their pets, but do not forget that uncontrolled breeding of cats leads to an increase in the number homeless animals. In addition to surgery, there are less radical ways to neutralize sexual activity in cats. A number of drugs have been developed that weaken sex drive, but before giving any of them to your pet, you need to consult your veterinarian. Quite different problems arise for those who purposefully intend to breed purebred cats. When choosing a partner for his pet, the owner should familiarize himself with the pedigree of the candidates, find out what their state of health is and what the previous offspring of the producer was, if the animal has already mated. Also, all necessary vaccinations should be made to potential partners

Chapter Nine: Breeding Your Angora Cat

in advance. Female domestic cats become sexually mature at the age of 12 months, cats much later, at 2 years old. Animals are ready to start breeding much earlier: females at the age of 6-8 months, males at the age of 8-10 months, however, early mating, and then pregnancy and childbirth weaken young animals, therefore the optimal age for the first mating 1.5-2 years. At a later age, various difficulties are almost inevitable.

Acquaintance and subsequent mating of thoroughbred animals usually occurs on the territory of the male. To make it easier for animals to establish contact, the owners can exchange any things of their pets in advance. Cats will get used to the smell of the future partner and will subsequently perceive it as something familiar and familiar. The owner of the female also needs to inspect in advance the place where the mating of animals will take place. Sometimes it happens that as a result stress caused by the move to the place of residence of the male, the female stops estrus. In this case, you should not put the cat next to the cat immediately. The animal must get used to the unfamiliar environment. The cat will quickly get used to and feel more comfortable with her favorite things - a bed for sleeping or a toy. When the cat feels confident enough, you can place it in a separate cage, but make sure that it can see the male. At first, the cat can behave quite aggressively. The animal hisses, bends back or, on the contrary, trying to hide. But this behavior is usually is one of the elements of mating games for cats. Animal behavior quickly changes: the cat flirts with the cat, then defiantly runs away from him. It is advisable to plant her with a cat just at such a moment when her favor for a partner is noticeable. For a more successful course of mating, it is preferable to select

Chapter Nine: Breeding Your Angora Cat

partners in such a way that at least one of them already has experience in mating.

Sometimes it may take a while for the animals to get to know each other. If they do not show aggression, you do not need to interfere with them, trying to speed things up. In healthy animals, the reproductive instinct is well developed, and if partners show interest in each other, there is no reason to fear that acquaintance will not have a positive result. Although sometimes it also happens that animals do not feel attraction to each other or even show aggression. In this case, the date will have to be interrupted. After a while, it will be possible to try to bring the cats together again. If the animals stubbornly do not want to communicate, they will have to find other partners for them. You need to knit cats only during estrus, since at other times it to do is pointless. Cats do not have such restrictions; they are ready to mate at any time.

Pregnancy

The cat's behavior after successful mating usually changes during the first days. The animal becomes less active, requires more attention from the owner, capriciousness and excessive pickiness in food, which is not characteristic of a cat, may appear. Some cats show unexpected aggressiveness early in pregnancy. Another indirect sign of pregnancy is seizures. called morning weakness, when the animal becomes very lethargic and lethargic. A pregnant cat's nipples turn pink, swell and gradually increase in size. They should be tense to the touch. During pregnancy, an animal's appetite

Chapter Nine: Breeding Your Angora Cat

can remain at the same level if the cat's diet contains sufficient amounts of essential nutrients and vitamins. However, it may increase, although a temporary loss of appetite is also possible. If your cat has a persistent loss of appetite, you need to consult a veterinarian. Pregnancy in cats lasts 63 to 68 days, although childbirth can occur as late as 59 days after conception. For childbirth, you need to prepare a place in advance. It is best to take a box of a suitable size, put a bedding inside and put the house in a secluded corner where the cat most likes to relax.

Childbirth

Behavioral change is a sign of impending labor. animal. The cat loses appetite, shows unreasonable anxiety and tries to hide. Special assistance during childbirth is very rarely required for animals, however, just in case, you need to prepare in advance everything that may be required to provide it. You should have a few clean towels, sterilized scissors, threads, iodine and a heating pad with hot water on hand. Kittens are born enclosed in an amniotic membrane, which the cat tears apart itself. It also gnaws at the umbilical cord and eats the placenta. Then the cat licks the cub. If the cat for some reason has not ruptured the amniotic membrane, the owner should do this as soon as possible, otherwise the kitten will suffocate. Between the birth of kittens takes from 30 minutes to 1 hour. If this process is delayed for a long time (3 hours or more), then you need to contact your veterinarian. After the end of the contractions and the cessation of labor, you need to carefully feel the cat's stomach and make sure

Chapter Nine: Breeding Your Angora Cat

that all the kittens have been born. Sometimes it happens that the baby remains in the uterus for some reason. In this case, the cat usually behaves restless. To provide an animal with qualified assistance, you need to call a veterinarian. Sometimes a kitten, partially already out, gets stuck in the birth canal. This happens when the contractions are weakened or when the calf is very large. You need to try to get the kitten out. This is done as follows. The cub should be wrapped with a clean gauze napkin or towel and, gently holding, gradually release from the birth canal of the cat. Then it is necessary to quickly rupture the amniotic membrane and clear the kitten's oral cavity of mucus.

Newborn kittens appear blind and deaf. Eyes open in about 7-10 days, kittens begin to see later, 12-20 days after birth. They begin to hear sounds a little earlier, 9-10 days after birth. Smell and touch are well developed in newborn kittens. Highly the cubs make attempts to move quickly. As a rule, a mother cat almost never leaves kittens unattended at first. If a particularly curious kitten tries to get out of the box, the cat immediately puts it back in place. You can determine the gender of newborns, after a simple inspection. You need to take the cub in your hand, raise its tail and carefully take a closer look at how the corresponding holes look. The topmost opening is the anus. In females, the vaginal opening located just below it looks like a vertical slit. In males, the distance between the anus and the testes is slightly larger, the testes look like two small swellings, directly below which is the opening of the penis.

Chapter Nine: Breeding Your Angora Cat

Raising Kittens

Often, cats that have a lot of milk willingly feed not only their own, but also other people's cubs. This quality of animals can use if kittens (a sometimes the babies of other animals, such as puppies) were left without a mother. During the period of feeding the cubs, the attitude of the mother cat to the outside world changes dramatically. Instinctively protecting kittens from potential danger, she becomes alert and aggressive. It is not recommended to disturb the cat and her cubs unnecessarily, but from time to time it is still advisable to clean her house. In addition, you need to monitor the physical condition of the cat and kittens.

Kittens grow very quickly. At the age of 3 weeks, milk teeth erupt. At the same time, animals begin to show significant activity, independently move around the box and the surrounding area and play with each other. Kittens at the age of 3-4 weeks, especially if there are a lot of them in the litter, you need feed with milk porridge, into which little by little meat, cut into small pieces, is added, and then vegetables. Kittens at the age of 5-6 weeks end the formation of the dental system, which allows them to eat more solid foods. At the age of 8 weeks, animals are recommended to be weaned from their mother and transferred to self-feeding. At first, kittens need to be fed 6 times a day in small portions, two of which should consist of dairy products, and the rest should be a variety of porridges with lean meat.

Chapter Nine: Breeding Your Angora Cat

Artificial Feeding

In some situations, there is a need for artificial feeding kittens. This happens if the cat has died or is seriously ill or has no milk. The best option, of course, is to put the cubs of the foster mother, but this is not always possible to do. In order to feed kittens, you need to comply with the necessary conditions. A safe and warm shelter should be prepared for the animals. For this a box with soft bedding will do the trick. You can also use a special house for a cat. In the room where the kittens are located, it is necessary to maintain a sufficiently high air temperature. In the first week of life of animals, it should not fall below 30 ° C; in the second week, its slight decrease is permissible. The next 2 weeks the air temperature should be 24-25 ° C. Animals need to be protected from drafts and sudden temperature fluctuations, as newborn kittens can easily get sick and die.

Recipes have been developed for special nutritional mixtures intended for feeding kittens. For example, Scott's Blend provides an animal with all the nutrients it needs to grow and develop. This mixture is easy to make yourself at home. To do this, you need to take 50 ml of natural cow's milk and mix with 15 g of powdered milk. Take 1 large chicken egg, separate the white from the yolk. Beat the protein in a mixer until a thick foam forms. Mix the protein and yolk with milk, add 1 ml of vegetable oil, 4 g of grape sugar and 2.5 g of dry food to the mixture yeast. Mix everything thoroughly until a homogeneous mass is formed. You need to feed kittens from a bottle with a nipple, which is necessary sterilize before each feeding. The first 2 days the kittens are fed every 2 hours,

Chapter Nine: Breeding Your Angora Cat

then the breaks between feedings are gradually increased to 3-4 hours.

Kittens should not be overfeeded, as an early habit overeating is one of the causes of obesity. Overweight animals develop worse and are more vulnerable to various diseases. Therefore, if the kittens refuse to eat the next meal, this is not a cause for concern. The animals may have overeat during the previous feed. In this case, you need to reduce the single serving of food. With normal development, kittens should gain 80-120 g in weight in a week. In newborn kittens, the excretory reflex is not sufficiently developed. The mother cat, licking the cubs, thereby stimulates its development. Kittens who are left without a mother need to regularly massage the anal and genitourinary openings with a damp cotton swab. If the kittens are constipated, an enema can be given. To do this, take a small syringe without a needle, the cone of which must first be lubricated petroleum jelly.

Conclusion

Angora cats are really excellent creatures and make for great pets to keep. If you have been a cat lover your whole life then you know what great pets they make. If you are looking for a different type of pet that can be loving and yet have some independence then an Angora cat can make for a perfect choice.

You do want to be sure to pick your breed carefully to be sure that you find a good match. Consider the type of cat that you want based on your lifestyle, if there are kids or other pets in the home, and if they are going to be left alone for a specific amount of time. There is always a cat that will make for a great fit, but you have to take the time to find the right one.

Angora cats do require a lot of care, but they are well worth the investment of time and money. They are very loyal and though they may not be around as often as a dog, they are going to love you unconditionally just the same. Do be sure that you know what you need to do to give your Angora cat everything that they need though, as this will make it a great experience for both pet and owner. These guidelines will help you to give your cat everything they want and need. You will show them love and it will be returned. Give them love and special attention, and you will have a loving pet for many years— Angora cats are great and now you can see firsthand!

Conclusion

Glossary of Cat Terms

Ailurophile- A person who loves cats.

Ailurophobe - A person who fears or even hates cat.

Allergen - In relation to cats, the primary allergen, the substance that causes an allergic reaction in some people, is, Fel d 1, a protein produced by the cat's sebaceous glands, and present in its saliva.

Allergy - A high level of sensitivity present in some people to a given substance, like the protein Fel d 1 in cats. Generally, the reaction includes, but is not limited to watering eyes, sneezing, itching, and skin rashes.

Alter - A term which refers to the neutering or spaying of a cat or dog.

Bloodline - The verifiable line of descent that establishes an animal's pedigree.

Breed Standard - A set of standards for a given breed formulated by parent breed clubs and used as the basis for evaluating show quality animals.

Breed - Term that refers to a group of cats with defined physical characteristics that are related by common ancestry.

Breeder - A person who works with a particular breed of cats, producing offspring from high-quality dams and sires for the purpose of maintaining and improving the genetic quality of the line.

Breeding - The process in which dams and sires are paired for the purpose of producing offspring.

Breeding Program - An organized and ongoing program in which cats are mated selectively to produce offspring that are ideal examples of the breed.

Breeding Quality - A term describing a cat that meets the standards of a given breed to a degree sufficient to be included in a breeding program.

Breed True - The phrase which describes the capacity of a male and female cat to produce kittens that closely resemble themselves in accepted elements of the breed standard.

Carpal Pads - Located on a cat's front legs at the "wrists," these pads provide added traction for the animal's gait.
Castrate - The medical procedure whereby a male cat's testicles are removed.

Caterwaul - A feline vocalization that produces a discordant, shrill sound.

Cat Fancy - Term used to describe the overall group of registered associations clubs, and individuals that breed and show cats.

Catnip - A member of the mint family, this aromatic perennial herb (Nepeta cataria) contains an oil to which some cats are strongly attracted and to which they respond with a kind of

Glossary of Cat Terms

"stoned" intoxication. Kittens cannot respond to catnip until they are 8-9 months of age.

Cattery - Any establishment that exists for the purpose of housing cats, and where they are bred as part of an organized program.

Certified Pedigree - A pedigree that has been issued in an official capacity by a feline registering association.

Clowder - A collective term for a group of cats.

Coat - Term referring to a cat's fur.

Crate - Container used to safely transport cats from one location to another or to confine them temporarily for their own safety.

Crepuscular - Although known in popular lore as nocturnal animals, cats are actually crepuscular, meaning they are most active at dusk and dawn.

Crossbred - A cat that is the product of breeding a sire and a dam of different breeds.

Dam - The female in a parenting set of cats.

Dander - The small scale of hair and skin that are shed by an animal. Often responsible for allergic reactions in individuals with a sensitivity to the substance.

Declawing - A highly controversial surgical procedure that removes a cat's claws permanently.
Desex - Describes the alteration of an animal by neutering or spaying.

Glossary of Cat Terms

Domesticated - Animals that have been tamed to live with or work with humans, or that have chosen to cultivate such a relationship.

Ear Mites - Microscopic parasites that feed on the lining of a cat's ear canal, causing debris to build up, generating a foul odor, and resulting in extreme itching.

Entire - A term describing a cat that has an intact reproductive system.

Exhibitor - An individual that participates in organized cat shows.

Fel d 1 - A protein produced by the cat's sebaceous glands, and present in its saliva, which causes an allergic reaction in some people.

Feline - A member of the family Felidae. Includes lions, tigers, jaguars, and wild and domestic cats.

Fleas - Various bloodsucking insects of the order Siphonaptera. They are wingless, and their legs are adapted for jumping. They are parasitical, and feed off warm-blooded animals.

Flehmening/Flehmen Reaction - A facial gesture in cats that is often mistaken for a grimace. In reality, the cat is drawing in air to pass it over a special structure in the roof of the mouth called the Jacobsen's Organ, which functions as a second set of nostrils and allows cats to "taste" a scent.

Glossary of Cat Terms

Gene pool - In a population of organisms, the "gene pool" is the collective genetic information relative to reproduction.

Genes - Determine particular characteristics in a given organism. They are a distinct hereditary unit and consist of a DNA sequence occupying a specific location on a chromosome.

Genetic - Refers to any trait, characteristic, tendency, or condition that is inherited.

Genetically Linked Defects - Health specific problems or those relative to temperament that are passed from one generation to the next.

Genetics - The scientific study of heredity.

Genotype - Refers to the genetic makeup of an organism or a group of organisms.

Groom - The act of caring for the coat of a feline, which may include brushing, combing, trimming, or washing.

Guard Hair - Long, coarse hairs that form the outer layer of a cat's coat.

Heat - The seasonal estrus cycle of a female cat (or any other mammal).

Hereditary - Any characteristic, trait, disease, or condition that can be genetically transmitted from parent to offspring.
Histamine - A physiologically active amine in plant and

Glossary of Cat Terms

animal tissue released from mast cells as part of an allergic reaction in humans.

Hock - Anatomical term describing the ankle of a cat's hind leg.

Household Pet - A cat not registered to be exhibited or shown in competition.

Housetraining - The process whereby a cat is trained to use a litter box to live cleanly in a house.

Humane Societies - Any one of a number of groups that work to put an end to animal suffering due to overt acts of cruelty and other impoverishing or harmful circumstances.

Immunization - The use of inoculations to create immunity against disease. Also referred to as vaccination.

Innate - A quality, trait, or tendency present at birth and thus inborn

Inbreeding - When two closely-related cats of the same breed are mated.

Instinct - A pattern of behavior in a species that is inborn and comes in response to specific environmental stimuli. Intact - Animals that are intact possess their complete reproductive system. They have not been neutered or spayed.

Jacobsen's Organ - An organ located in the roof of a cat's mouth that allows it to "taste" a scent. Appears as two small openings and is regarded as a second set of "nostrils."

Glossary of Cat Terms

Kindle - A collective term for a group of kittens. An alternate term is "chowder."

Kitten - Young cats under the age of 6 months.

Lactation - Process by which the mammary glands form and secrete milk.

Lactating - Term used for a mammalian mother when she is secreting or producing milk.

Litter - The number of offspring in a single birth. Generally 3-4 in cats, although 6-10 is not uncommon.

Litter Box - A container filled with commercial kitty litter or sand and used in the home as a sanitary and manageable location for a cat to urinate and defecate.

Longhair - Cats with varying lengths of long hair, typically with plumed tails and prominent neck ruffs.

Mites - Small arachnids (of the order Acarina) that are parasites on animals and plants. Often seen in the ears of felines.

Moggy - The term for a mixed breed cat in the United Kingdom.

Muzzle - In cats, the part of the head projecting forward including the mouth, nose, and jaws. May also be referred to as the snout.

Neuter - The term used to describe castrating a male cat.

Glossary of Cat Terms

Nictitating Membrane - A cat's third eyelid, which is a transparent inner eyelid that serves to protect and moisten the eye.

Nocturnal - Term used to describe animals that are most active at night. It is mistakenly applied to cats, who are actually crepuscular, being most active at dawn and dusk.

Odd-Eyed - Eyes of two different colors presenting in a single individual.

Papers - The documentation of a cat's pedigree and registration.

Pedigree - A cat's genealogy presented in writing and spanning three or more generations.

Pet Quality - A cat that does not sufficiently meet the accepted standard for its breed to be shown in competition or to be used in a breeding program.

Queen - An intact female cat, one that has not been spayed.

Quick - The vascular portion of a cat's claw that will, if clipped, bleed profusely.

Rabies - A viral disease that is highly infections and typically fatal to warm blooded animals. It attacks the central nervous system and is transmitted by the bite of an infected animal.

Recognition - The point at which a cat breed is officially accepted under a cat fancy organization's rules. Registered

Cat - A cat registered through a recognized feline association that has documentation of its ancestry.

Glossary of Cat Terms

Registered Name - The official name used by a registered cat, which is typically long and reflective of its ancestry.

Registration - The record of the particulars of a cat's birth and ancestry filed with an official organization.

Scratching Post - A tower-like structure covered in carpet or rope that allows a cat to sharpen and clean its claws inside the house without being destructive to furniture.

Secondary Coat - In a cat, the fine hairs of the undercoat.

Semi-Longhair - Long-haired cats with a medium-length coat.

Shelter - Any local organization that exists for the purpose of rescuing and caring for homeless and stray animals. Also works to find permanent homes for these animals.

Show - An organized exhibition in which judges evaluate cats according to accepted standard for each breed and make awards accordingly.

Show Cat - Cats that participate in shows. Show Quality - Cats that meet the standards for their breed at a sufficient level to compete in organized cat shows.

Show Standard - A description of the ideal qualities of a breed of cats used as the basis for which the cats are judged in competition. Also known as standard of point.

Sire - The male member of a parenting set of cats.

Spay - The surgery to remove a female cat's ovaries.

Glossary of Cat Terms

Spray - A territorial behavior typically seen in male cats whereby the animal emits a stream of urine as a marker.

Stud - An intact male cat that has not been altered and is used as part of a breeding program.

Subcutaneous - Placed just below the skin, as in an injection.

Tapetum Lucidum - The interior portion of a cat's eye that aids in night vision and is highly reflective.

Undercoat - The layer of a cat's coat that is composed of down hairs.

Undercolor - The color of the hair lying closest to a cat's skin.

Vaccine - A weakened or dead preparation of a bacterium, virus, or other pathogen used to stimulate the production of antibodies for the purpose of creating immunity against the disease when injected.

Wean - The point at which a kitten begins to eat solid food and is taken off its mother's milk as the primary source of nutrition.

Whisker Break - Refers to an indentation of the upper jaw on a cat.

Whisker Pad - The thickened or fatty pads on either side of a cat's face holding rows of sensory whiskers.

Whole - A cat of either gender that is intact, and has not been neutered or spayed.

Index

A

adopt 7
age 29
aggression 74
appetite 123

B

bathing 42
bed 15
behavior 85, 122
breed 2, 114, 118
breeder 6, 8
brushing 40

C

car 76
certification 91
chewing 72
children 27
claws 38
clicker 55
coat 40
collars 13
color 4, 114
come 56
contract 11

D

disease 87
diseases 95

E

ears 40
environment 19

exercise 84

F

feed 29
feeding 24
feline 15, 95
female 121
females 114
fertilization 119
flap 47
fleas 82
food 17
frequency 35
fur 3

G

genetic 4
genital 12
groom 18
grooming 37

H

hairballs 41
health 11, 80
home 9, 13, 19

I

illness 85
insurance 92
interaction 5

K

kittens 123

L

leash 63
litter 11, 46

litter box 14

M

male 121
males.. 114

N

nail 38
name 50
neutering 83

P

paw 59
paws... 7
plants 22
pregnancy 122

Q

quantity... 35

R

reproduction 120

S

scratching.. 16, 72
select... 8
show.. 113
sit 53
skin 37
spaying 83
stand 54
stay.. 53
stress... 71

T

ticks 82
tomcat... 119

toys 13, 17
training 49, 68
traveling 76
treat 53
trimming 38

U

urine 71

V

vaccinations 81
veterinarian 11, 35
veterinarians 89
vision 12
vitamin 34
vitamins 82

W

water 86

Photo Credits

Page 2, Jupiterimages via Canva.com (Canva Pro License)

https://www.canva.com/photos/MAC8TQ13-n8-turkish-angora-cat/

Page 8, Esin Deniz via Canva.com (Canva Pro License)

https://www.canva.com/photos/MAEFE-adxIg-turkish-angora-cat/

Page 13, vimart via Canva.com (Canva Pro License)

https://www.canva.com/photos/MAEAci-CBEw-portrait-of-cute-turkish-angora-cat/

Page 29, Yulia_Mozes via Canva.com (Canva Pro License)

https://www.canva.com/photos/MADBDerUkQo-angora-cat/

Page 37, Oleg Baliuk via Canva.com (Canva Pro License)

Photo Credits

https://www.canva.com/photos/MAEX6Xbr8Cw-veterinarian-trims-cat-s-claws/

Page 45, vimart via Canva.com (Canva Pro License)

https://www.canva.com/photos/MAD_51h-R3w-portrait-of-cute-turkish-angora-cat/

Page 80, Oleg Baliuk via Canva.com (Canva Pro License)

https://www.canva.com/photos/MAEX6Uc-N2E-vet-checks-eyes-of-a-white-cat/

Page 113, Instants via Canva.com (Canva Pro License)

https://www.canva.com/photos/MAEJcyHc4rc-turkish-angora-cat/

Page 118, viewbug via Canva.com (Canva Pro License)

https://www.canva.com/photos/MADqSLtQaNA/

References

Turkish Angora – Dailypaws.com

https://www.dailypaws.com/cats-kittens/cat-breeds/turkish-angora

Turkish Angora - Petfinder.com

https://www.petfinder.com/cat-breeds/turkish-angora/

Turkish Angora Cat Information and Personality Traits – Hillspet.com

https://www.hillspet.com/cat-care/cat-breeds/turkish-angora

Behavior And Care Of The Turkish Angora Cat - Hospitalveterinariglories.com

https://www.hospitalveterinariglories.com/turkish-angora-cat/?lang=en

Turkish Angora: Cat Breed Profile - Thesprucepets.com

https://www.thesprucepets.com/turkish-angora-cat-breed-profile-4774070

The Turkish Angora – Pethealthnetwork.com

https://www.pethealthnetwork.com/cat-health/cat-breeds/turkish-angora

Turkish Angora - Vcahospitals.com

References

https://vcahospitals.com/know-your-pet/cat-breeds/turkish-angora

Turkish Angora - Vetstreet.com

http://www.vetstreet.com/cats/turkish-angora#1_o00c0agb

Turkish Angora Cat Breed - Purina.com

https://www.purina.com/cats/cat-breeds/turkish-angora

Turkish Angora – Animalhealthcenternh.com

https://animalhealthcenternh.com/client-resources/breed-info/turkish-angora/

Meet the Turkish Angora - Pumpkin.care

https://www.pumpkin.care/cat-breeds/turkish-angora/

About the Turkish Angora - Cfa.org

https://cfa.org/turkish-angora/

Turkish Angora: Cat Breeds – Madpaws.com.au

https://www.madpaws.com.au/blog/turkish-angora/

How To Identify An Angora Cat - Animals.mom.com

https://animals.mom.com/how-to-identify-an-angora-cat-12312400.html

Breed Profile | Turkish Angora – Petprotect.co.uk

References

https://www.petprotect.co.uk/blog/breed-profile-turkish-angora-cat/

Turkish Angora - Holidogtimes.com

https://www.holidogtimes.com/cat/cat-breeds/turkish-angora/

Turkish Angora Cats– Petinsurance.com

https://www.petinsurance.com/healthzone/pet-breeds/cat-breeds/turkish-angora/

Turkish Angora - Catbreedslist.com

https://www.catbreedslist.com/all-cat-breeds/turkish-angora.html

Turkish Angora Cat - Rabbitmatters.com

https://www.hepper.com/turkish-angora-cat/

Turkish Angora Cat- Allaboutcats.com

https://allaboutcats.com/cat-breeds/turkish-angora

Turkish Angora Cat Breed Traits and Profile - Cats.lovetoknow.com/

https://cats.lovetoknow.com/cat-breeds/turkish-angora-cat-breed-traits-profile

References

www.ingramcontent.com/pod-product-compliance
Lightning Source LLC
LaVergne TN
LVHW051835080426
835512LV00018B/2896